WHEELER

WHEELER

by Esther Fraser

A Summerthought Publication
Box 1420, Banff, Alberta, Canada

ISBN 0-919934-07-2

First Edition, 1978

Published by
Summerthought Ltd.
P. O. Box 1420
Banff, Alberta T0L 0C0
Canada

Printed and bound in Canada

Foreword

When Esther Fraser's *The Canadian Rockies: Early Travels and Explorations* was published in 1969, it was welcomed by all who possessed an interest in this mountain range. Since that time this work has sold some 20,000 copies and has become an important sourcebook for the early history of the Canadian Rockies. Regional writers always have a thumb-worn copy close at hand. Journalists from around the world have drawn upon it extensively in writing of the area. A whole new generation of writers and scholars have been stimulated to delve more deeply into the lives of the characters revealed in this popular history.

Not long after the publication of *The Canadian Rockies*, Esther began her own research into the life of one of the region's historical figures. Out of the many colourful and significant individuals she might of chosen, it may seem curious that A.O. Wheeler was selected. Having spent much time working over the manuscript with Esther prior to publication, I no longer find the choice unusual. Not only did Esther realize the pivotal role which Wheeler played in both the exploration and development of the Rockies—particularly in the region's definition as a recreation area and wildland preserve—but I am certain she came to identify strongly with the dynamic and indefatigable personality of her protagonist, the courage and devotion of his first wife Clara, and the strength and vitality of Emmeline Savatard. In my association with her, I came to recognize many of these qualities in Esther herself.

It is a pity that Esther could not have lived to see the publication of this book. We can only speculate as to other important works she may have embarked upon had she lived. Yet, together with *The Canadian Rockies, Wheeler* will stand as an important contribution to the understanding of the early history of European exploration and settlement in the mountain west. For myself and other writers of the region, Esther Fraser will remain an important pioneer in the field of Rocky Mountain literature—a great lady of the mountains.

Brian Patton
Banff, 1978.

Prologue

Late in 1907 Arthur Oliver Wheeler visited England as an honoured guest of the prestigious Alpine Club of London. It was a highlight in the life of one of Canada's most colourful pioneer surveyors.

At forty-seven he was a well-muscled man of medium height with auburn hair, neatly trimmed beard, moustache, greying sideburns, and dark eyes sparkling with good humour. Handsome in carefully chosen formal dress, he took his place at the head table two seats removed from the Club President, The Lord Bishop of Bristol. With urbane self-assurance, he chatted with Lord Alverstone, Chief Justice of England, who had adjudicated the Alaska-Yukon Boundary question which Wheeler had investigated on the spot in 1903.

A few months before this auspicious European vacation he had completed a season of field work in the mountains of British Columbia where, with characteristic vigour and satisfaction, he had slashed trail with his crew through virgin forests, packed heavy photographic equipment and instruments to summits, strode long miles in stifling heat tormented by blackflies and mosquitoes, enjoyed "comfy" evenings with his men after twelve-hour days, and camped in snow-filled meadows.

The dinner celebrating the Jubilee of the Alpine Club was held at Oxford in the historic hall of Lincoln's Inn; with immense satisfaction Wheeler noted that this "remarkable gathering" was distinguished by the presence of representatives "of the Church, the State, the Navy, the Army and the Sciences and all the learned professions . . . stars, orders and ribbons" showing that many had "made their mark in their respective callings." For generations Wheeler's ancestors had "made their mark" in all those fields of endeavour. In1790 his grandfather's brother, Sir Jonah Denny Wheeler-Cuffe, First Baronet, had read law in this building.

A few weeks later Arthur disembarked on Ireland's shore at night and walked until daylight to a high point of land above Dublin Bay. Below, the water glistened between winter's bare branches of beech and ash; in the moist soft distance the clouds of dawn drifted over gentle mountains—the remembered hills of his boyhood. Strolling back to Kingstown, a suburb of Dublin, he "looked up the house where we lived and the old bathing place". He had spent happy summers there with parents, aunts, uncles, brothers, sisters, and cousins.

1

In Dublin he went to Sunday service at St. Patrick's Cathedral where the great master of English prose, Jonathan Swift, was appointed Dean in 1713. Swift was friend and admirer of the most illustrious of Arthur's ancestors, Dr. Richard Helsham, M.D., Senior Fellow, Lecturer of Mathematics, and Professor of Physics at Trinity College, Dublin; his *Lectures on Natural Philosophy* was a textbook at Trinity for nearly a century.

Next day Arthur travelled to ancient Kilkenny City; walking along its narrow streets he found St. Canice's Cathedral serenely crowning a little hill. In this thirteenth century church the founder of Wheeler fortunes and influence in Ireland, Lord Bishop Jonas Wheeler, is interred "under a fair Marble Monument".

He called on the Rector of St. Mary's Church with which his mother's family, the Helshams, had been associated for centuries. As Registrar and Librarian of dioceses including St. Canice, he was able to show Arthur a piece of its antique Communion plate which his mother had asked him to see, The Wheeler Flagon. With a silver foot, handle, lid and neck, its elaborate engravings include "the royal arms of Elizabeth", a Wheeler crest, and faded date letter for 1587-88. Fashioned from a polished cocoanut traditionally said to have been brought back to England by Sir Walter Raleigh, it was presented to Bishop Wheeler when "Her Majesty Queen Elizabeth of Glorious memory" made him Dean of Christ Church, Dublin, in 1594. As Royal Chaplain to the Great Elizabeth he could have enjoyed security and promotion in England but chose to risk the possibility of greater rewards in Ireland. Arthur would have been delighted to know that his ecclessiastical ancestor had been a bit of an adventurer.

In the evening, wandering beside the river Nore, Arthur saw the imposing turrets and bastions of Kilkenny Castle silhouetted against the stars; since the fourteenth century it had been the home of the illustrious Butler family, the Earls of Ormonde. Members of the British Royal family were often house guests there; and Arthur's mother and father had attended receptions in its famous picture gallery which occupies the entire eastern wing.

A solicitor took him a few miles beyond the city to Mount Brilliant and Glendine. His grandfather and father had spent their early years on these estates—estates which Arthur would inherit. Hiring "a jaunting car", he took the well-remembered drive two miles south-east of Kilkenny to the estate of his father's cousin, Sir Charles Frederick Denny Wheeler-Cuffe, Second Baronet. Principal seat of the Wheeler-Cuffes since the early eighteenth century, stately Lyrath House was as picturesque as ever, in its setting of rolling acres with fast-flowing stream, waterfalls, and ruined hill fort.

Still on the family estate, he stopped at a gem of a Georgian country house beautifully situated on the river Nore. The Rocks—the house where he was born.

Arthur and his cousin and host, Colonel Edward Oliver Wheeler, had grown up here. When Colonel Wheeler inherited the house he made extensive restorations but Arthur slept in the room where he had read—and dreamed of adventure in far-off Canada.

He was not a sentimental man, but pride of race and family bonds were strong. The flood of memories evoked by his nostalgic visit brought a sharp realization of how painful it must have been for his parents to wrench ancient roots and leave for Canada thirty-two years before.

Chapter I

Arthur Wheeler's parents, Captain Edward Oliver Wheeler and Josephine Helsham, were born into the ruling class of Ireland. Landed gentry of English origin, families like the Wheelers, Cuffes, and Helshams enjoyed the social, economic, and political influence which enabled them to govern even though they were a tiny Anglican minority threatened by the Roman Catholic majority.

Bishop Wheeler, as an agent of Tudor religious policy, came to Ireland to strengthen the weak Protestant establishment. He did this to his sovereigns' satisfaction although some of the lands he "recovered" were probably expropriated from the native Irish. The Anglo-Irish Establishment owed their supremacy to the peace imposed by Cromwell's armies and the merciless seizure of Roman Catholic property.

Bishop Wheeler's son, Oliver, as a Lieutenant-Colonel in Cromwell's army, received a grant of land and held a seat in the Restoration Irish Parliament in 1661. Forty years later his descendant was granted lands and an ancient castle, Lyrath, in County Kilkenny. He built a new house, part of which is incorporated in the more pretentious late-Georgian building erected by the First Baronet, Sir Jonah Denny Wheeler-Cuffe, in the lifetime of his younger brother, Captain William Oliver Wheeler, Arthur's grandfather.

Like other "young men of means and good family" (one was the Honourable Arthur Wellesley, later the Duke of Wellington), William Oliver Wheeler bought a commission in the crack cavalry regiment, the 12th Lancers, which was fighting Napoleon in Portugal and Spain when Arthur's father, Edward Oliver Wheeler, was born. In 1829, William Oliver Wheeler was Mayor of Kilkenny. With his wife, Mary Helsham Wheeler, he enjoyed to the hilt the rollicking carefree life of the Irish landed gentry.

This was the kind of life Arthur Wheeler's father hoped to live. However, as the second of William Oliver Wheeler's six sons, Edward Oliver Wheeler would inherit only a small part of the Wheeler estates, the major portion going to Sir Jonah's heir. Edward Wheeler would have to find some means of supplementing his income.

His father bought him a Captain's commission in the Kilkenny Fusilliers. In his thirties he was photographed in the smart dress uniform, probably on one of the occasions when he was presented at Court, either at St. James or Dublin.

Family legend insists that, at some time before 1850, Arthur Wheeler's father came to Canada where he married a daughter of the Honourable Thomas Parke, a member of the Upper Canada Legislative Assembly. His wife died, probably in childbirth. The death of the child a few years later added to the tragedy and Edward Wheeler returned to his father's home at The Rocks.

At forty-four he married his second cousin, twenty-four year old Josephine Helsham, whom he had probably met on one of her visits to her Irish relatives. The Helshams were also an eminent Anglo-Irish family. As a Cromwellian officer, Arthur Helsham received a grant of land and a castle in County Kilkenny in 1652. Like the Wheelers, succeeding generations of Helshams acted as Members of Parliament, High Sheriffs, Justices of the Peace, and Mayors, and some were distinguished ecclesiastics. Josephine's father, Dr. Arthur Helsham, was born in Kilkenny but before 1815 had a medical practice in London where he acquired considerable property. As a "gentleman born", he would continue family custom by occasionally donning knee breeches, silk stockings, sword, and Court costume to make his bow to the Sovereign at St. James' Palace.

In their four-storey terrace house, with liveries, servants, and carriages emblazoned with the Helsham arms, Dr. Helsham and his very proud wife, Elizabeth, raised a family of three sons and two daughters.

Josephine, the youngest child, was very well educated. She was fluent in German and French, read Italian, and had a good grounding in history. Obviously she had inherited the Helshams' strong intellectual bent, a gift nourished by her father. When she accompanied him in his carriage on visits to country patients, she read aloud to him from the books he treasured and he encouraged her comments and discussion.

In her twenties she was tall with a regal bearing, a delicate complexion, finely-arched nose, auburn hair, and a soft, very pleasing Irish voice. Her marriage to Captain Edward Wheeler took place October 28th, 1857, in London's very fashionable church, St. George's, Hanover Square.

They then moved to Dublin where Edward waited upon the Lord Lieutenant and officials, hoping to secure a position in the Irish Establishment. He failed and moved to The Rocks to administer his aged father's estate.

In that spacious house their eldest son, Arthur Oliver, was born on May 1st, 1860, followed at two-year intervals by sisters, Hester and Kathleen, brothers Richard Denny, William, and five years later, Hector. There, too, Edward and Josephine Wheeler spent the happiest years of their lives.

While her husband led the only kind of life he ever found congenial, Josephine was delighted with the gay social whirl involving a cluster of prominent families living on nearby estates. The grandest of these was Desart Court, home of the illustrious Cuffe family — the Fourth Earl of Desart was Edward's fox-hunting friend. One of young Arthur Wheeler's earliest memories must have been of the great occasions when his parents, elegant in evening dress, left in their carriage to dine from the famous gold plate at Desart Court.

Ever since Edward's great grandfather's marriage to a niece of the Right Honourable John Cuffe, First Baron Desart (an alliance which greatly enhanced Wheeler fortunes and influence), the Wheelers considered themselves

*Josephine Helsham Wheeler and Captain Edward
Oliver Wheeler, parents of A. O. Wheeler.*

a branch of the Cuffe family and close relationships were maintained between Desart Court and Lyrath House.

The renown of the Cuffes exceeded that of the Wheelers and the arrival of the first Cuffe from England in 1599 was decidedly more flamboyant than the clerical mission of Bishop Wheeler. Henry Cuffe, Oxford scholar and teacher, accompanied that impetuous and ambitious favourite of Queen Elizabeth, the Earl of Essex, when he went to quell Tyrone's rebellion. Essex failed. Cuffe had been his agent in Ireland and had tried, without success, to have him reinstated at Court. Just before his execution Essex blamed Cuffe for "all these my disloyal courses...." Cuffe proclaimed innocence when brought to trial himself, but was dragged to Tyburn and hanged.

However, another branch of the family flourished in Ireland as Cromwellian officers and members of Parliament and in 1733 the peerage was conferred on John Cuffe, First Baron Desart.

Young Arthur would have gone with his family to visit at Desart Court. When the carriage swept to a stop on the graceful driveway amid the bustle of footmen, the doors of the classical two-storey central block would be thrust wide. In a great confusion of welcoming handshakes, the guests would be ushered into the spacious hall which was hung with family portraits. Two semi-circular passages led to the wings which accommodated children and guests. At the back of the house two superb double staircases led to bedrooms and a "noble gallery" above the very large drawing room. In this room, gay with chintzes, the smell of sweet peas, roses, and wet dogs, there was "a pianola which some child was always playing."

For generations booted, spurred, and brilliantly uniformed men had danced in this "grand baronial mansion" before marching off to war; here, loved ones had wept and, with tears of gratitude, welcomed heroes home. In massive beds wives had writhed in pain to give birth to sons and heirs. Old men and women had died. And at least one gentle illegitimate boy had spent brief years there.

Arthur would have sat at the huge oval table in the dining room with as many as twenty guests, while at one end the Earl carved a succulent leg of mutton or beef and his Countess served "the fowls" at the other. From the drawing room windows, he looked out at the gently undulating parkland dotted with its woods of great oaks. There he, Bessie, Hester, Kathleen and Richard Denny roamed and rode. Especially fascinating for the boys was the stable yard, the saddle room redolent of old polished leather, the cobbled yard where carriage horses waited in their loose boxes, and the Earl's splendid hunters.

With what excitement he waited as a small boy for the return of uncles, cousins, and father from the day's hunt! And, later, how thrilling for an adolescent to ride with them: bright red jackets milling, yelping hounds, the hot sheen of the horses' hides...the trained animal's quivering impatience...green fields and woods streaming past...the satisfaction of controlling your magnificent beast—all the dash, colour, and drama so beloved by outdoor squires.

Captain Wheeler and Josephine's children would not always accompany them on week-long visits to the splendid old homes of relatives and friends, but The Rocks must have been lively enough with the presence of three cousins and their widowed mother, servants, a genteel governess, and Arthur's venerable great aunt, Elizabeth, Lady Cuffe, who left Lyrath House when her husband, Sir Jonah, died. Arthur may have remembered his grandfather, William Oliver Wheeler, who lived at The Rocks until his death when Arthur was three. Of course Arthur's parents offered unfailing hospitality at The Rocks, although not in the boisterous style of which Arthur's grandfather boasted. In *his* day the success of a party was judged by the number of male guests the host could drink under the table.

When Arthur was home from his schools in Dublin and Ballinasloe, County Galway, he would occasionally go with his father when rents were collected on the 1738 acres the Wheeler-Cuffes owned in the 1870s. Edward Wheeler's elder brother had died, leaving an heir underage; he acted as his guardian and administered the estates, and probably also those of his cousin, Sir Charles Frederick Wheeler-Cuffe, the Second Baronet, who served as Brigadier Major at Malta and fought in the Indian Mutiny before returning to Lyrath. Captain Edward Wheeler's younger brothers had already emigrated to Australia so he temporarily assumed the position of head of the family, taking on the responsibilities and privileges of a landed gentleman by acting as County Magistrate.

On excursions over the estates, father and son were sometimes pelted

"The Rocks"

with eggs by protesting tenants. Captain Wheeler took this all with Irish good humour. Landlords are seldom popular and he was none too exacting, or even efficient; it was said that he often gave away more to the needy than he collected.

When Arthur was fourteen he entered Dulwich College, London—a distinguished old school considerably transformed by a century of great educational reform. With emphasis on the classics, "playing the game", devotion to sports—Kingsley's "muscular Christianity"—it was one of those institutions whose object was to produce an elite of young gentlemen with a serious approach to life's work, trained for the universities, professions, and civil service. In the last three decades of the nineteenth century these schools were caught up in the enthusiasm for Imperialism and students were strongly motivated by a "mission to Empire". Graduates with this moral fervour did, like Arthur Wheeler, make significant contributions as civil servants in Queen Victoria's Empire.

By 1876 Captain Edward Wheeler's circumstances had changed drastically. A glut of agricultural products in British markets caused an alarming crash in prices with consequent rural unemployment and a sharp decrease in rental income. Hardest hit were the landowning aristocracy, especially small squires like Arthur's father whose inheritance consisted of two estates, Mount Brilliant and Glendine. Being unsuccessful in finding means to supplement his income, he had undoubtedly been living beyond his means for years, and his nephew, for whom he had acted as guardian, was now of age. Captain Wheeler's growing family could not expect to live on at The Rocks. The only avenue open to him was to sell the life interest in the estates which would provide a lump sum for repayment of debts and a move to a new country.

In this crisis he turned to his friend, the renowned Sir James Edward William Theobald Butler, Third Marquess of Ormonde at Kilkenny Castle, who not only bought the life interest in the estates but sent personal testimonials to Lord Dufferin, Governor General of Canada.

Letters had been exchanged with Canadian officials which indicated, or were construed to mean, that the Captain's military background and county administrative experience would qualify him for a post with the recently formed North West Mounted Police. His thoughts turned to Canada for several reasons: he had been there earlier; a cousin had married Sir John Glover who was appointed Governor of Newfoundland in 1876; and Josephine's sister, Catherine, had married and spent some years in Toronto during the 1850's. But the death of Josephine's father in 1875 decidedly facilitated the move to Canada; his will substantially increased the income from her dowry and this was crucial, for Mrs. Wheeler's income largely supported the family until they reached maturity.

Josephine's last months in Ireland were pathetic. Knowing that she was cutting all ties with her role as Lady of the Manor, she hoarded every scrap of evidence pertaining to those happy years and placed them in her wedding scrapbook. This she bequeathed in her will to her eldest son as a reminder of his heritage. Included is the account of the last great event to which she and her husband were invited: the wedding of the Marquess of Ormonde to the eldest daughter of the Duke of Westminster. Ironically a death in the Duke's family sent them into mourning and the event in Kilkenny Castle took place privately. But included in the imposing list of those sending gifts (which was headed by Queen Victoria) were those of Captain and Mrs. Edward Oliver Wheeler and a Wheeler cousin and friend of Josephine's, Minnie Cochrane, who was Lady-in-Waiting for H.R.H. Princess Beatrice, youngest daughter of Queen Victoria.

Some of Josephine's precious wedding gifts and heirlooms were sold to provide additional capital and early in the spring of 1876 the family embarked for Canada. As their ship steamed slowly out into the Atlantic and headed toward the western horizon, Josephine and Edward watched the coast of Ireland fading into the distance—forever.

For Edward Oliver Wheeler at the age of sixty-three, the journey was a desperate step into an uncertain future. For forty-three year old Josephine it was an ordeal. Facing for the first time the care of six children without assistance (Bessie, the eldest, had remained in England for a year) and expecting her eighth child, the prolonged sea voyage must have seemed interminable. An early thaw littered the ocean with menacing icebergs, forcing the ship to seek a more southerly route.

When they reached Ottawa on May 14th, they moved into a Sparks Street hotel, where the very next day Josephine gave birth to her last child, Josephine Helsham Wheeler.

Only bitter disappointment awaited Captain Wheeler. No position was available. Probably his age ruled out the post with the N.W.M.P. but it is possible that politics were involved. At a time when patronage was dispensed with unabashed partiality, the Liberal government of Alexander Mackenzie was unlikely to consider with favour a man who unfailingly proclaimed that he was "a red hot Tory"! However, even at this distance, the recommendations of the Marquess of Ormonde carried weight and he was offered a sinecure position as harbour master of Collingwood, Ontario.

Chapter II

Travelling to Collingwood by train, the Wheelers found themselves in a thriving small town hugging the rim of Georgian Bay and sheltered on the west by the timbered ridge of Collingwood's Blue Mountains. The arrival of the railway in 1855 had made it a major transportation terminus and the harbour was picturesque with an impressive array of masts.

On Minnesota Street, Captain Wheeler leased an attractive and commodious white house, The Birches. The first floor consisted of a walnut-panelled hallway, very spacious dining room, large drawing room with doors leading to a glassed-in conservatory, a morning room, and a kitchen. The drawing room was handsomely furnished in Victorian fashion with a piano, tapestry-covered chairs, a few small heirlooms, family photographs, and potted palms. Upstairs were a large master bedroom suite with a nursery attached and five other bedrooms; the large attic served as a bedroom for the boys. While the grounds could not compare to the rolling acres of The Rocks, they were extensive, with large kitchen and flower gardens, lawns, root house and, at a considerable distance from the house, the stables, though the Wheeler income no longer allowed the expense of horses and carriage.

Captain Wheeler took up his not too arduous duties and Josephine shouldered the burden of running a household with only one assistant, an inexperienced farm girl hired for five dollars a month. A family of similar financial standing, the Hamiltons, had a maid "who couldn't milk, bake or wash". Mrs. Wheeler's girl could not cook and Wheeler daughters said their mother insisted on being locked in the kitchen to force herself to learn how to feed her family. Garden produce had to be harvested and preserved, water brought from the well, stoves which heated all the rooms had to be supplied with coal and wood. Arthur and his brothers and sisters undoubtedly shared many of these chores and probably benefited from a new family cohesiveness.

Like many settled Eastern communities, Collingwood's residents were very class conscious. "Society" was of course less exalted than that to which the Wheelers were accustomed, but the upper echelons of the hierarchy consisted of families whose backgrounds made them congenial. There was Mayor George Moberly, son of a Royal Navy officer who had married a member of Polish aristocracy; Mrs. George Moberly came from a very old and distinguished Irish family. W. B. Hamilton's family had a pedigree which included the Dukes and Earls of Hamilton; Dr. Stephen, a town physician, was a son of Lady Brickenden; and at the pinnacle of the social scale was the great Dr. Lett, graduate of Trinity College, Dublin, and rector of All Saints Anglican Church.

Mrs. Wheeler courteously received the social calls of the prominent ladies but it was generally felt that she had "retired from society", whether because of pride (springing from a feeling that if one could no longer entertain as Lady of the Manor, then it had best be done as sparingly as possible) or because she was overwhelmed with home and family responsibilities. But her husband was a gregarious man and she was a gracious hostess; as the children matured, The Birches was often lively with parties of family friends.

The young Wheelers revelled in the novel experiences of Canadian winters: toboggan sliding, skating, long snowshoe tramps to surrounding hills. Bessie, Arthur, Hester, and Kathleen joined gay young people and adults to skim over snowy trails in trim cutters as horses' bells rang in frosty night air—they were on their way to exclusive parties at The Batteaux, the elegant country home of two English gentlemen, situated on a hill overlooking the town.

The school which Arthur's younger brothers and Kathleen attended had eleven teachers when the Wheelers arrived. Like Arthur, Richard Denny and Hector developed keen minds and Kathleen showed literary talent. In a few years they were putting out a small newspaper which gently lampooned their neighbours and referred to people and events in their parents' circle with some irony. The Wheeler children had been brought up with a sense of their social ascendancy and it is significant that they should treat their parents' friends with irony. Arthur, with longer exposure to the aristocratic life (supplemented by his Dulwich schooling), only tempered his traditional social attitudes later.

Arthur was faced with the immediate and vital choice of a career, one which could be provided by the family's diminished means.

He often "went with Pater to his weekly Whist Club" whose members would be predominantly, if not exclusively, members of All Saints Anglican Church and the Conservative party. In those days that type of all-male gathering inevitably included spirited discussion of politics, and whatever Canadian history Arthur had studied at Dulwich became more vivid as these staunch supporters of former Prime Minister Sir John A. Macdonald assessed the issues of the day.

With typical partisanship, the economic depression would be attributed to the weakness of Alexander Mackenzie's Liberal government. A whole decade of brilliant nation building by Sir John was threatened by the lack of effective action so characteristic of his over-cautious successor. British Columbia, which had been lured into Confederation in 1871 by the promise of a transcontinental railway, was threatening to secede. If the threat became a reality the whole immense extent of the North West from Lake Superior to the Rockies would follow British Columbia's lead and fall into the eager hands of the Yankees. Sir John had forseen that danger during the Red River uprising in 1870 when he dispatched Colonel Garnet Wolseley's Expeditionary

"The Birches," Collingwood, Ontario.

Force to Fort Garry. A show of force near the International Boundary had certainly demonstrated that the North West would not be yielded as readily as the Oregon Territory in the treaty of 1846.

But that was just a temporary and tenuous measure. The North West would be secure only when it was firmly linked to the eastern provinces and British Columbia by rail. And building sections here and there, what progress was the present government making with *that*? The one hope was that Sir John would soon be back in power. He had already announced an election platform including protective tariffs to revive the economy and early completion of the railway which would be paid for by settlement of the North West.

Would settlers go to the almost unknown and isolated North West? The Wheelers' friend George Moberly of Collingwood maintained they would. His brother Walter was in Winnipeg and reported that the southern part of the tiny new province of Manitoba was a land of boundless promise for settlers. Good arable land was nearly all taken up in the eastern provinces and depression was forcing foreclosure on many mortgaged farms. Settlers were beginning to trickle west. George Moberly could offer further reliable evidence about the feasibility of building the Transcontinental and settling the North West.

Walter Moberly had been employed by Sandford Fleming Engineer-in-chief of Sir John's first Canadian Pacific Railway) when Fleming made his epic journey from the Atlantic to the Pacific in 1872, and the Moberlys had read with keen interest the popular account of that trip. The gifted diarist, Reverend George Grant, who had accompanied Fleming, published the record of the expedition under the title *Ocean to Ocean*. Like many others, George Moberly believed that anyone who read Grant's book would have no doubts about the future of the North West.

Walter Moberly's career as surveyor-explorer was a colourful one. After working on the Ontario, Simcoe and Huron Railway he explored extensively north of Lakes Huron and Superior. Meeting the celebrated "wandering artist," Paul Kane, he was captivated by tales of adventure in the North West, and went to the Pacific where he helped to build the famous Cariboo Road to the gold fields. In 1860 he met Captain John Palliser, whose far-ranging expedition had explored the plains from Lake of the Woods to the Rockies. Challenged by Palliser's conclusion that there was no possible rail route through the barrier of the Selkirk and Gold Ranges, he set out to prove otherwise and discovered Eagle Pass through the Gold Range.

In 1871 Fleming hired him to locate the proposed rail line between the Shuswap Lakes and the eastern foothills of the Rockies. He set out on the day British Columbia joined Confederation, and was soon convinced that he had succeeded in his mission to find the best route through the mountains: follow the Big Bend of the mighty Columbia River around the impenetrable Selkirk Range from Revelstoke to Golden and cross the Rockies via Howse Pass. But Fleming meticulously continued to send his surveyors to probe every conceivable pass through the mighty ramparts of the Rockies.

Accounts of Moberly's exploits strengthened Arthur's cherished ambition for adventure. But what had aroused this "boyhood dream"?

When Arthur was twelve years old, a member of the illustrious Butler family published a very popular book about his travels in Canada's wild and virtually uninhabited North West. Undoubtedly Arthur had read it. Its vivid descriptions were the source of the young boy's longing for adventure in that remote, romantic country.

The Great Lone Land—the very title was hauntingly poetic. A country of "immense inland seas [and] mighty rivers whose waters seek their mother ocean through three thousand miles of meadow"; in those rivers "the red man steers his little birch-bark canoe down foaming rapids" and the solitudes are "broken only by the whisper of the pine tree and the music of running water... The prairie-ocean of grass... whose shores are the crests of mountain ranges eternally capped with snow...." No Victorian boy with a drop of adventure in his blood would fail to be moved by its ringing phrases.

A fortunate destiny had placed Arthur on the very fringe of the Great Lone Land. Was it possible that he could help to extend the course of Empire westward, fulfill his boyhood dreams of adventure and, at the same time, satisfy the immediate needs for a practical profession?

Consultation with a son of the Wheelers' friends, the Hamiltons, confirmed Arthur's hopes. With the inevitable settlement of the North West and the construction of the railway, surveyors would be in demand. The dashing, experienced surveyor, Lauchlan Alexander Hamilton, eight years older than

Arthur, was in partnership with Collingwood's George Urquart Ryley, and Arthur enlisted with their firm as apprentice surveyor. Hamilton's prediction was sound; his own career and subsequent work with the Railway was to be a brilliant success and his association with Arthur continued far beyond the short apprenticeship.

To qualify as Dominion Land Surveyor required mastery of the first six books of Euclid, knowledge of plane and spherical trigonometry, mensuration of superficies, astronomy, geology, plotting and map making, the keeping of field note books, and the use of instruments in practical surveying experience.

In the spring of 1877, Arthur heard that another Collingwood surveyor, Elihu Stewart, was taking a small party for a summer of field work in the Algoma district on the north shore of the Great Lakes.

In his copy of *The Great Lone Land* Arthur found the inspiring half-remembered passages: "…great lonely lakes…the inland ocean of Superior…. It is worth looking at, the world possesses not its equal…one vast spring of purest crystal water, so cold, that during summer months its waters are like ice itself and so clear, that hundreds of feet below the surface the rocks stand out as distinctly as though seen through plate-glass." The opportunity to realize "a boyhood dream to go up the Great Lakes and spend the summer in a birch-bark canoe" was irresistible. Mr. Stewart accepted him as an apprentice.

In Collingwood's harbour, he boarded "the old-time side-wheeler, the *Frances Smith*", the gangway was raised and they steamed out into the calm of Georgian Bay, the northeastern arm of mighty Lake Huron. Passing into the North Channel, they stopped at an Indian settlement on Manitoulin Island where Arthur saw their birch-bark canoes—the canoes which, to Butler, looked like "yellow leaves of autumn" floating on the river.

Sixty-three years later A. O. Wheeler wrote that in 1877 he had "spent the summer, much of the time in a birch-bark canoe, exploring…," and like Butler's "red man" he discovered that the frail craft was like a "high-mettled charger which will do anything if he be rightly handled." Those exhilarating days marked the beginning of his prowess with the paddle which led to the challenge of canoe racing, and life-long skill and pleasure with that craft.

It was a memorable summer for other reasons too. North of the Lakes on the rugged Laurentian terrain, 1,383 acres of mineral lands were sold that year, and Mr. Stewart's party surveyed lots into parcels of 320 acres for settlement. At the time there were only "a scattering of settlers in isolated houses erected in a clearing". More than half a century later, on a boating and camping vacation on Shuswap Lakes, A. O. Wheeler sat beside the campfire with his only grandson. With youthful admiration for the rugged pioneer whose clear complexion, white hair and neat goatee glowed in the firelight, the very young boy asked "Grandad, what was the *toughest* trip you ever made?" The answer was immediate: "My very first summer in the bush, north of Bruce Mines…"

Sometimes Mr. Stewart would send him out as a scout, a day ahead of the rest of the party. It was all very well for a man in the prime of life, with Butler's experience in wilderness travel, to write glowing prose about a land "where loneliness lives so thoroughly". To read with boyish thrill a romantic account of treks in "the lonely grandeur" of the "trackless forest" was strikingly different from experiencing the reality for the first time.

For hours young Arthur walked on the hump-backed hills of primeval rock, with their covering of jagged pines where the unfathomable black lakes—haunts of wild geese and loons—mirrored the gloomy conifers. As night closed in he extinguished the last embers of the fire where he had boiled water for tea in his frying pan before baking bannock and frying bacon in the same utensil. He curled up in his blanket—and listened to the solitude. Every rustle of dead leaf, each soft movement of a tiny nocturnal animal, roused the primitive tingle of fear. But fear was vanquished. During a long life some of A. O. Wheeler's deepest emotions and sense of achievement were experienced in moments of solitude and physical danger.

Chapter III

Since 1871 the Government had negotiated treaties with the Indians of the North West, and some of the chiefs were anxious to have their reserves surveyed. In 1878 Elihu Stewart had a contract to survey reserves near Prince Albert in today's province of Saskatchewan, and Arthur Wheeler accompanied him.

This time they crossed the whole expanse of Superior; taking a lake boat to Duluth, they proceeded by rail through the United States to Moorehead where they embarked on one of the old steamboats which churned its way through the turgid Red River to Winnipeg. In that bustling community of seven thousand the party was outfitted, and Arthur learned what was involved in preparing for a long trek into the western hinterland. It took days to buy Red River carts, horses, tents, cook stove, blankets, waterproofs, tools, clothing, guns, ammunition, medicine chest, soap, toweling, cooking utensils, crockery, and food. Then each cart had to be systematically loaded to avoid delays in setting up camps. With Mr. Stewart's cart carrying the all-important surveying instruments, the little brigade set its course westward.

According to Wheeler's notes "the entire distance from Winnipeg, over six hundred miles, was made on foot..." In those days surveyors' allowances were too meager to cover the cost of extra saddle horses.

The Carlton Trail, which they followed, skirted the wooded Assiniboine River, passed the little village of Portage La Prairie and "the farthest outpost, the little town of Brandon, 135 miles from Winnipeg"; the next stage was to Fort Ellice and up the wide and beautiful valley of the Qu'Appelle River to Fort Qu'Appelle, where the N.W.M.P. had established a post the year before. The route then ran northwest toward the Touchwood Hills, descended the western side and crossed what was called the Great Salt Plain toward the Quill Lakes. Ascending from this plain, travellers approached the south and north branches of the Saskatchewan River.

For Arthur Wheeler this field trip was not just another step in his apprenticeship. He was following Butler's course into the Great Lone Land and, like Butler, he experienced "days of unceasing travel from dawn to dusk" which took him into its solitudes; he saw Butler's "prairie-ocean...a vast expanse of grass and pale pink roses...."

During six weeks of travel Arthur did indeed discover the delight of spreading a waterproof on the grass-scented floor of his tent and the luxury of slipping between two blankets to enjoy the rest of a bone-weary man. But often heavy spring rains made the trail almost impassable; crossing flooded creeks, climbing out of coulees and the high banks of the Assiniboine required strong muscles to help slithering horses regain their footing. Descending steep hillsides, the track was deep-rutted, strewn with boulders and half-exposed roots. Even the sturdy Red River carts were not impervious and axles snapped. Hefty axemen had to fashion new ones out of felled trees.

But there was also the sheer joy of bathing in clear fresh pools, of shooting wild fowl which feathered willow-fringed lakelets. There was the exhilaration of striding through the uncut sea of grass as dawn bathed the vast expanse in golden light, and the evening rest round cheering campfires while the blood-red sun sank beneath the level ring of the ever-distant horizon.

From a western spur of the Touchwood Hills the party saw an immense empty plain stretching into space. No drinkable water or wood for fuel existed there, so a twenty-four-hour supply had to be carried in the carts. The Great Salt Plain was awful in its desolation, criss-crossed by deeply-scoured buffalo tracks and littered with bleached skulls of the mighty beasts of the plain.

With great relief the isolated little caravan ascended a range of grassy hills where woods encased sparkling pools and meadows were ablaze with prairie wildflowers. When they climbed the last ridge and saw the magnificent panorama of the South Saskatchewan River, they knew they were at last reaching their destination. The Hudson's Bay Company ferry took their outfit across the river; at Fort Carlton the north branch was easily crossed, and on August 17th they reached what Mr. Stewart refers to as "the Sturgeon Lake Indian Reserve of the Prince Albert Settlement".

His crew began the survey at once, "according to instruction," but were delayed when the Cree Indians were "not satisfied with the way I was instructed", and it was not until "they had interviewed His Honour Lieut. Governor Laird and had succeeded in getting the reserve extended farther west on the south side of the lake than was originally intended that I was enabled to meet their views on the matter."

With the season now well advanced, the surveyors returned to Prince Albert Settlement, at the time a scattering of about five hundred people in "settlements extending from Fort Carlton to the junction of the North and South branches of the Saskatchewan." Here they were to lay out two reserves on the South Saskatchewan. Again work was well underway when the chief returned and expressed dissatisfaction over land allotted. After careful consultation Stewart decided "to jog my line far enough south to include the portion they wished to occupy".

By acceding as far as possible to the Indians' wishes, Stewart was adhering to government policy. The Red River uprising in 1869-70 had been partly caused by the arrival of surveyors who, on government orders and without consulting or even advising the inhabitants of their intention, began dividing the Metis settlers' traditional ribbon-like farms into the tidy squares or sections.

Stewart's report does not say when the field work was finished, but it must have been in the late autumn of 1878. Another famous surveyor, J. S. Dennis (with whom Wheeler would serve in a quite different venture in a few years), worked in the Battleford area that year and his report states that the party finished work on "October 4th and arrived in Winnipeg November 5th after a most disagreeable journey."

Stewart's party made the return trip in five weeks and it is highly probable that during that time they weathered at least one early snowstorm. If so, it would have been Árthur Wheeler's first experience under canvas in the snow. After more than five months in the North West he was tanned, fit, and well-muscled, and he had acquired the surveyor's typical long, easy, evenly paced stride.

Arthur Wheeler was to make his greatest professional contribution in western Canada, but when he returned to work there after an absence of three years, the west had been transformed.

The winds of change swept across the Dominion in the next decade. Faint intimations were evident when Elihu Stewart's party returned from the field. A railway ran from Winnipeg south to the United States border. Donald A. Smith, Member of Parliament for Selkirk, had persuaded the government in Ottawa to complete this line. By the end of 1878 it was connected at Pembina with the American St. Paul and Pacific Railway which Smith owned in partnership with his cousin George Stephen, President of the Bank of Montreal. As Arthur Wheeler returned to his studies in Collingwood, Smith, Stephen, and partners began to reap the enormous profits yielded by the St. Paul and Pacific.

John A. Macdonald had swept back into power with a landslide victory in 1878 and set out to fulfill his election promise to link Canada from the Atlantic to the Pacific with a railroad and settle the North West. Even though economic depression had eased, the staggering cost of building the line seemed beyond the government's means. Would it be cheaper to run it across the southern prairies rather than along the recommended northerly route following the fertile belt of the North Saskatchewan? Were the prairies suitable for settlement? Sir John wanted more information about the North West and in 1879 he dispatched ten parties of surveyors to prepare reports for him. One of the men he sent with them was Professor John Macoun—a man who would shortly assume a very important role in Arthur Wheeler's life.

In 1872, when Sandford Fleming's party was westward bound on its journey from "ocean to ocean", the enthusiastic activities of botanist John Macoun aroused Fleming's interest. At every point where their steamer docked on the Great Lakes "the first man on shore was the Botanist, scrambling over the rocks or diving into the wood, vasculum in hand, stuffing it full of mosses, ferns, liverworts, sedges, grasses and flowers till recalled by the whistle that the captain always obligingly sounded for him."

Forty year old Macoun was assiduously adding to his botanical collection, and when Fleming asked him to join their expedition he accepted on the spot even though it would mean an eight-month absence from wife and family and his teaching position at Albert College, Belleville, Ontario. The lure of thousands of miles of virgin botanical grounds was compelling.

As the voyage on the lakes continued, Macoun was "in raptures over sundry rare mosses and beautiful specimens...." Soon he had fellow passengers in his wake, leading them "a rare chase over rocks and through woods...quite indifferent to the toil or danger." With yells of triumph he would summon his followers to "come and behold the treasure he had lit upon. They would find him on hands and knees 'before some thing of beauty' that seemed to them little different from what they had passed by with indifference thousands of times." Nonetheless, his enthusiasm was captivating and soon "almost every one of the passengers was bitten with 'the grass mania'...."

His fervour remained undiminished when, at Fort Edmonton he left the main expedition on Fleming's instructions. "Bidding them adieu", he turned on his heels with a "Hurrah for the Peace River!" He would soon "settle the problem of its disputed fertility"!

It was an incredibly rigorous and dangerous trek, during which he went on foot to Fort St. John, through the mountains by Peace River Pass, and to Fort McLeod where he made an eighty mile dogsled journey to Fort St. James, sleeping outdoors in below-zero temperatures. In knee-deep snow he continued to Quesnel where the stagecoach took him over the Cariboo Trail to Yale and from there he canoed to New Westminster. He sailed to San Francisco and returned home to Belleville by train. The report he wrote of his findings was included in Sandford Fleming's Railway Report of 1874.

In 1875 Dr. Selwyn of the Geological Survey was going to the Peace River country, and according to Macoun, Selwyn insisted that he "must have that man with me." Alexander Mackenzie's government was in power and the staunch Conservative Macoun thought politics might make him unacceptable. But a friend pointed out that "no one else [was] so well fitted for the position." With unabashed self-confidence Macoun reported that "it turned out as he had said."

On the eight month, eight thousand mile journey he went from California to Victoria ("which should be the Garden of Canada!") and retraced northward the steps of his 1872 trip to Fort St. John. When other party members "cursed the road and black flies, I in my simplicity, saw nothing but Nature decked out in springtime loveliness...." He marvelled at the luxuriance of crops and gardens at the fur trade posts at Hudson Hope and Fort St. John. After gruelling days living on mouldy pemmican and tea, he was escorted on the long journey to Fort Carlton by Hudson's Bay Company men and Indians.

Travelling by cart over the old route to Winnipeg, he stayed behind on the roadside one morning to write up his notes. Engrossed with thoughts of all the rich potential of the country he had seen, he "became poetical and had just written: 'I think I hear the tramp of the coming millions' when a concert broke out a few yards behind me, and on looking round, I saw a line of coyotes sitting on a ridge and giving rise to their peculiar howl. I need scarcely add that I never became poetical again!"

When he arrived in Winnipeg in November, he displayed the barley and wheat he had picked at Fort Chipewyan and told all who would listen of the wonderful country he had passed through.

On the last lap of his homeward journey he went by stage to Fargo, North Dakota. When the sleigh tipped, spilling passengers in the snow, all able-bodied men hastened to rescue two ladies who were "of course, screaming as loudly as possible." No-nonsense Macoun ordered the rescuers to right the sleigh first. "I said, what proved to be the truth, that ladies who could scream like they were doing, could not be badly hurt"!

At public lectures in Ontario he spoke with tremendous enthusiasm of the vast rich territories awaiting settlers, and as he "always enunciated opinions with great force," it was most frustrating that "Prime Minister Mackenzie

Wedding portrait of Mr. and Mrs. John Macoun.

would not believe one word I told him about the Northwest." However, his report was again included in Fleming's 1877 Railway Report, and when Sir John returned to power and sought "general knowledge of the prairie country," Macoun resigned from his position at Albert College and went to Ottawa where he talked to Fleming and Sir John's Minister of Railways, Dr. Charles Tupper. As a result of the meeting Macoun went to explore the southern prairies.

In 1879, accompanied by a surveyor, he went to Fort Ellice, on to Battleford, and along the "Blackfoot Trail" to the Red Deer River, Fort Calgary, and "Old Bow Fort at the entrance to the Rocky Mountains." When he returned to Winnipeg via Fort Edmonton he found "great changes...a large number of influential men" were there now and he lectured to one thousand: "I was just in a condition to fill them full because I was in a state of more than common excitement....I fearlessly announced that the so-called arid country was one of unsurpassed fertility...."

Travelling through the southern plains from Brandon to Cypress Hills the next summer only confirmed his views, which he vigorously defended even from the visitors' gallery in the House of Commons. His lectures to large crowds (in Ottawa, Governor General, the Marquess of Lorne, was in the audience) "caused much excitement amongst adventurous people throughout the country..."

Influential people were indeed listening to John Macoun. Dr. Tupper began to believe that he was "not merely proclaiming the guesses of an ill-informed enthusiast." If there really were so many millions of acres of arable land south of the fertile belt of the North Saskatchewan, would it be cheaper to build the line there? Would settlers prefer the less wooded land because it would be easier to cultivate? And would the sale of lands help to cover the cost of railway building?

J. J. Hill of the St. Paul and Pacific Railway had heard and read Macoun's appraisals of the prairies. Hill and his partners R. B. Angus, George Stephen, and Donald Smith had formed what came to be known as "the Syndicate" and were ready to invest the millions they had garnered from their formerly bankrupt Minnesota railway. When Sir John decided to look for entrepreneurs to take over the colossal task of building the Transcontinental, the Syndicate made a bid for the charter. It was accepted by the government, and early in 1881 the Canadian Pacific Railway Company was incorporated.

A few weeks later Macoun, on Hill's invitation, met Stephen, Hill, and Angus in St. Paul and assured them that "an easy road could be made from Moose Jaw to Medicine Hat"; furthermore, he had looked up the wide valley of the Bow River two years before and was positive that it would provide a perfectly feasible route through the Rockies. The decision to span the North West and the Rockies by a southern route was made on the spot. The C.P.R. established its western headquarters in Winnipeg, and the first sod of the prairie section was turned at Portage La Prairie on May 2, 1881. The swift metamorphosis of the North West was about to begin.

Arthur Wheeler witnessed the frenzy of activity which radiated from Winnipeg. By the time he qualified as Ontario Land Surveyor in 1881, Lauchlan Hamilton had moved to a good position in the Timber, Mines and Grazing Division of the Department of the Interior, and in that year he and his survey partner George Ryley worked out of Winnipeg on a contract to allot land for permits to cut railroad timber. These timber limits had to be surveyed, and Arthur qualified as Manitoba and Dominion Land Surveyor during the two years spent on this work.

Winnipeg seethed with action and the exhilaration of growth; prosperity and change were in the air. Cut timber joined the tons of supplies hauled daily by a steady stream of trains to supply-depots along the ribbon of steel building westward. Millions of dollars were being spent on new buildings and homes; fortunes were made—and lost—in a day. 1881 and 1882 were Winnipeg's boom years when land speculators descended like a plague of locusts. John Macoun was right. There was "much excitement amongst adventurous people throughout the country." Railway construction drew them like a magnet.

In 1882, when Arthur Wheeler returned west for the season's field work, the C.P.R.'s dynamic new General Manager, William Van Horne, was preparing to lay an unprecedented number of miles of track. Hordes of men, responding to his relentless demands for swifter progress, swarmed like bees at the end of track which daily crept a few more miles across the prairie.

Collingwood's Lauchlan Hamilton had joined the C.P.R. and was surveying these new towns. Early in 1882 he was appointed Assistant Land Commissioner for the railway and was earning the very handsome annual salary of $2400. It is possible that during those boom years he began to build the foundations for the fortune he would amass before he retired. George Ryley had taken over his post with the Department of the Interior and Wheeler worked on surveying timber berths for him. When he returned from the field at the end of the season's work, the end of track was beyond Regina.

The trickle of settlers grew to a flood in 1883, and twenty-three year-old Wheeler was one of the record number of surveyors working that year when an astonishing 27 million acres were staked for settlement.

This was the first time he was in charge of a party and it was a heavy responsibility. With the isolated group of nine men hired in Winnipeg, Wheeler worked and lived for six months in a land many people have found unbearably lonely—the prairies south of Moose Jaw, Saskatchewan. Friction was bound to develop and Wheeler must have exhibited qualities of leadership. As another surveyor said about his "chief", he was the one "who must be obeyed". He had to earn the respect of the men under him, and his natural amiability probably won their friendship as well.

Making their way to the International Boundary, then north-west to today's Assiniboia area and west to Kincaid, they located and measured specified townships. In his field notebooks he recorded the vital information: sketch maps, quality of soil and grass, wood and water resources. When they left, the virgin land was marked with surveyors' stakes.

This work was essential; orderly settlement was impossible until the task was completed. To accomplish it, pioneer surveyors endured severe hardships.

Travelling, camping and working near the boundary, Wheeler's party scoured the desolate land for willow brush and buffalo chips—there was no other fuel for their cooking fires. As they moved on and summer came, they worked for monotonous days when searing heat waves shimmered over dessicated grass and drinking water came from stagnant alkaline lakes. On the unprotected empty plains, work was often impossible: "Wind blowing a hurricane. Couldn't work all day." They were without food for a day when the man sent to Moose Jaw for supplies was delayed.

But from high coulee-scoured ridges they looked out onto vistas of endless grasslands, and once they experienced some of the excitement of the old romantic West when they hunted a small herd of buffalo and a tiny band of Sioux Indians visited their camp.

Part of the return journey to Winnipeg was probably by train, for by that time the railway had been thrust into the heart of the Rockies. The grossly inflated balloon of Winnipeg's boom and "Manitoba Fever" had been followed by depression; a killing frost ruined crops and the number of settlers dropped drastically. There was little demand for surveyors for the next season but Wheeler took a party to the Quill Lakes area in Saskatchewan where they marked township boundaries for the Department of the Interior. Fortunately he was able to work as well for Lauchlan Hamilton, "sub-dividing along the line of railway."

In August Hamilton went to the Pacific with Van Horne where the Railway's General Manager selected Vancouver as the western terminus. In 1885 Lauchlan Hamilton stood at Hamilton and Hastings Street West; behind him were his transitman, leveller, rodman, chainman, picketman and axemen. As the bronze plaque affixed to a building on that corner states: "In the silent solitude of the primeval forest he drove a wooden stake in the earth and commenced to measure an empty land into the streets of Vancouver."

William Frances Butler had "seen a sunset over the prairies...a great golden mist, a big river flowing from it, a dark herd of buffaloes slowly moving across the prairie distance to drink at the river...." When he returned in 1871 immense reaches of the Great Lone Land were "silent and deserted—the Indian and the buffalo gone, the settler not yet come."

Arthur Wheeler had seen the prairie sunsets and the remnants of the vanished buffalo. He had seen the settler come and the Indian hemmed in. But he had not seen, as Butler had, what lay beyond the portals of the setting sun: the great range of mountains, "the rugged magnificence of their glaciers and ice valleys...."

He returned to Ontario to train in a special branch of his profession, unaware that this training would take him to those mountains. And even as he was leaving the North West, the native people were planning one last act of violent protest against onrushing civilization which was banishing forever their wild free way of life.

Chapter IV

Immediately after the New Year festivities in Collingwood, Arthur left for Ottawa and his new position as "Third Class Clerk" in the Department of the Interior. Within a few weeks he moved upstairs to the office of the Surveyor General of Canada, Dr. Edouard Deville. the years he was to spend in that office were the ones during which Deville was studying, testing and improving the techniques which led him to introduce the camera as a surveying tool in Canada.

The mountains had challenged the railway pathfinders and builders; the terrain was also a problem of some magnitude for the surveyors. Deville believed that photo-topography could solve it. The relatively new technique would save time, an important consideration in terrain where conditions suitable for surveying last for only a few months. Fewer men would be required and they would spend less time in the field as the map-making could be done later. He developed special light-weight cameras and instruments which were much less cumbersome than plane-table apparatus, and easier to keep stable in the winds so often encountered on high stations. Deville's work proved to be so succesful that Canada, especially in the late nineteenth century, used the survey camera over areas unexceeded by any country in the world. Wheeler was to be one of the handful of pioneers in this work.

It was a stimulating time to be advancing in his profession and very satisfying to be establishing himself in Canada's capital city. He rented a room at Mrs. Gallup's house on Wellington Street and arranged to have his meals in good nearby hotels. After work he went for two-hour "constitutionals," and there was much to see: the icy cascades on the rivers, the beautiful view of the Gatineau Hills, streets of fine homes, and the impressive Parliament Buildings on the Hill. It was exciting to be working in those buildings where he encountered in the halls Members of Parliament, Senators, and the Prime Minister. He also saw them at the famous Russell Hotel.

Arthur quickly formed friendships with colleagues and young people who participated in vigorous outdoor sports. When the snow lay in great glistening mounds under stately trees, he sent home for his "furs" and went on long snowshoe tramps on the rivers. He joined the Ottawa Athletic Club and enjoyed tobogganing at "the Tache Slide" where evenings ended with "a fine lark" at someone's home—young ladies from Ottawa Ladies College could attend the slide parties if they had permission from the headmistress. Soon his social life included attendance at the Royal Museum Theater (where the Governor General and his wife were often patrons,) skating parties, and a weekend at Montreal's Winter Carnival where he did very well in competitions.

The young bachelor was delighted with his new life but also retained established habits: going to church service twice on Sundays and writing long letters to his mother. His professional status was modest and yet within weeks of his arrival he "went to write my name on the books at Rideau Hall" and a few days later was "presented to the Marquess and Marchioness in the Senate Drawing Room." This is the Arthur Wheeler with a long family tradition of being in touch with life at Court.

In February his seventy-two-year-old father came for a leisurely and enjoyable six-week visit and Arthur paid his expenses. Captain Wheeler immediately took his son to sittings of the House of Commons, called on Sir John A. Macdonald and "interviewed Sir David McPherson", Minister of the Interior. Edward Wheeler still had considerable presence and continued to "wait on great men." Undoubtedly the interviews were intended to advance his son's career, for on Arthur the family pinned all hopes of restoring Wheeler fortunes. The year after their arrival in Canada, Captain Wheeler made his will which left all of the family property to him. The other sons did not get a penny.

At twenty-five Arthur was dashingly handsome and obviously enjoyed feminine reaction to his charm. All the Wheeler brothers had this quality, especially Willie. At Collingwood skating parties, the debonair Willie would glide up to a bevy of young ladies and announce nonchalantly, "Next please"! There was never a shortage of volunteers for this privilege from demure damsels waiting on benches. After six weeks in Ottawa Arthur was being showered with invitations from Victorian mothers of marriageable daughters—and sometimes from the more venturesome daughters themselves.

These agreeable activities were interrupted by the shattering news of rebellion in the North West. In late March black headlines in the *Ottawa Citizen* filled front pages with stories about Riel's rebellion on the Saskatchewan: "Indians Scalping Settlers", "Settlers Besieged by Red Skins", "Foul Murder", "War Fever at Height."

Canada's young men were off to war. On March 30th the railway station in Toronto swarmed with families and sweethearts. They waved the first contingents an emotional farewell.

As in the earlier Red River uprising, the Rebellion sprang from the discontent of the Metis people. Hoping to escape the white man's encroachment, they had settled along the Saskatchewan between Prince Albert and Saskatoon. Their grievances were real. The buffalo were gone and drought had thwarted their attempts at farming. They and the Indians were starving. They also wanted title to the land they were occupying, land which the Dominion Government was surveying. When repeated pleas to the Government went unheeded, Louis Riel was recalled from exile in the United States to press their demands. Superintendent of the N.W.M.P. Crozier, sent an urgent telegram to Ottawa, warning that violence was imminent, and General Middleton's force of militia and volunteers were dispatched to quell the rebellion. Before

24

Middleton's Troop started west, Crozier's force of police and volunteers met in an unplanned encounter with Metis under Riel's able military commander, Gabriel Dumont; Crozier was forced to retreat with nine of his ninety-nine men killed.

On April 1st Arthur attended a meeting of surveyors held to discuss the possibility of organizing a "Surveyors Corps to go to the North-West Rebellion. Being only 25 years old and keen for anything that smacked of adventure, I promptly arranged to attend." What he failed to mention in his account, written fifty years later, was the surge of patriotism evoked by his decision to enlist. The Riel Rebellion aroused this sentiment in many Canadians—it was the first time the united Dominion had engaged in war. For a young man schooled to serve Her Majesty's Empire, the call to arms would be felt with particular force.

The Minister of Militia wired General Middleton who approved the formation of the Dominion Land Surveyors' Intelligence Corps of fifty. With experience in the North West, the surveyors could provide valuable information "as to trails and routes, and generally to act as intelligence men, or as scouts or mounted rifles...." The unit was to consist of ten Dominion Land Surveyors who had experience in the North West, and each of these was to recruit "four of the best assistants they had had."

Young Wheeler must have had an air of command and organizational ability. When the Corps came to elect "a Captain in command to handle the organization" he was their first choice. He declined immediately, feeling he had much less experience than others. J. S. Dennis was appointed. All the D.L.S. were ranked as lieutenants—a most expeditious way to earn a commission! —and the assistants as sergeants.

Arthur and his colleagues were given a farewell oyster supper; he had his photograph taken at Notmans and sent it to his mother with his personal belongings.

There were gaps in the C.P.R. tracks north of Lake Superior but Van Horne had promised to get the troops to Qu'Appelle in eleven days. He got the first contingents to Winnipeg in only four days but it was a gruelling trip, crossing those gaps in open sleighs and ploughing through deep snow in frigid temperatures. The D.L.S. Corps escaped this ordeal. "The Minister, desirous that we should reach the front as soon as possible decided to send us through to Winnipeg as civilians, via Chicago, Minneapolis and St. Paul." They went in a "special Pullman" and their "passage was a luxurious one...Had a jolly good time. Music and singing."

On April 14th they went into training in camp at Qu'Appelle. They had no distinctive uniform but wore slouch felt hats with a red flannel band, black leather jackets, white canvas bandoliers with haversack, cord riding breeches, and top boots. Their spurs were the most important part of the uniform: "your esteem in the troop was regulated by the length and quality of your spurs." The food was chiefly "sowbelly, bully beef, hardtack, coffee, tea and sugar", which their quartermaster, "a prince of foragers", supplemented on occasion with "a tender calf, a succulent pig or plump chickens".

The horses which were supposed to be ready for them had not arrived so Captain Dennis went to Regina and brought back a "fine lot of bronchos, some unbroken and real dandys." Happily, Wheeler got "a sturdy little sorrel."

Ready to go to the front, Dennis wired Middleton and on his orders proceeded to Swift Current to report to General Laurie in command there. On the morning of the 20th they detrained and had their first mounted parade. This, as Wheeler says, "was interesting".

Another participant described the scene. When the Captain gave the order: 'Pre-pare-to-mount! Mount!' some of the troopers get up so rapidly that they fall over on the other side; some crawl like a boy up a greased pole....Here a horse...pivots round and round on his own axis, and many signify their distaste for riders by bursting from line like lightning...bucking strenuously... We are about as disorderly a lot as one could care to see... Some were really good riders but a great many would have felt much safer on the ground where, indeed, several were violently deposited during the first encounter with their chargers."

Order was restored and Wheeler writes that "some bright brain conceived a quick, safe method of gentling bronchos. They were taken to a nearby slough and put through their paces in the soft mud around the edge. It was a dirty process, but effective." Wheeler was, of course, an excellent horseman and undoubtedly thought that this drill was remarkably different from those of his grandfather's crack cavalry regiment!

The incident which occurred a few days later might well have evoked a similar comparison. "Camp was pitched on the open prairie...and two sentries marched back and forth about the square." General Laurie and an aide called to inspect the troop and were promptly stopped at the lines and asked for the countersign. This he did not know, so said, 'It's all right, my man. I'm the General in command of this division.' The sentry: 'Halt and give the countersign!' The General: 'It's all right, I tell you.' The sentry: 'Halt!' The General, turning to his aide: 'Oh, come on!" The sentry: 'Halt, or I'll shoot!' The aide: 'I think he means it General. Better send for the officer of the day.' This was done and all was well." This became one of the General's favourite stories with which he regaled fellow officers later.

"A contingent from Quebec was in camp at Swift Current and the commanding officer was training it in tactics on the open prairie. The advance guard was seen from our camp, in open order, crawling on their stomachs up the slope of a long ridge. It was suggested to our Captain that it would be excellent practice for our mounted corps to suddenly appear from beyond the ridge as attackers, so we were promptly mounted, and taking a wide detour, gained a strategic position on the opposite side of the ridge. Spread out in a line, at the word 'Charge!' we drove in our spurs and went at it, hell for leather. In a moment we were over the top at a gallop and right amongst the crawling infantry, brandishing empty revolvers and yelling like demons." The startled troops dropped their rifles and "surrendered". The surveyors then dashed "down upon the main body [but] the officer in command was not so easily routed...He had drawn up his men in a solid body behind a long shallow slough. Through this we dashed, sending water flying in every direction, and were met by a wall of fixed bayonets and drawn swords, which most effectively broke the charge. We then joined up, shook hands, and had a good laugh with the honours even all round."

These were the hi-jinks of men eager for battle. Marching orders were received April 21st but changed and the Corps spent ten days at Swift Current acting as pony express riders carrying despatches to the forces in the field. It was rumoured that "Riel had skipped around Middleton's rear" and they were to be on the lookout for fugitives.

On April 23rd Middleton's forces had been fought to a standstill by Dumont's Metis at Fish Creek; on May 3rd the D.L.S. Corps was ordered to proceed to the battlefield at Batoche. Greatly relieved to be on their way they rode hard, camping in wet snow at nights. On their arrival in Saskatoon, ("then composed of a few log buildings"), they saw the men who had been wounded in the Fish Creek engagement.

At one of the Corps' camps on the way to Clarke's Crossing, Wheeler was officer of the day and "had gone out after dark to see that none of the sentries... were asleep. Searching the sky-line with my glasses, I saw, clearly silhouetted on a nearby ridge, the figure of a horseman coming towards me along the trail. I squatted down behind a willow bush and, as he came abreast shouted, 'Hands up!' The rider, in a very scared tone of voice, yelled: 'Hold on man! Don't shoot! I'm Howard, Gatling Howard!' His cavalry cap and U.S. army uniform declared his identity, so I took him to camp."

He was "Capt. Howard, an American army officer, detailed to operate a gun purchased from the Gatling Gun Company for the occasion. He explained that he was bringing his gun down with the streamer, which, owing to low water, was frequently stranded on sand bars, requiring much hard work to be hauled off again. He had tired of the monotony of it and had landed with his horse and set out to find our camp. We saw much of him during the campaign, for he frequently used our camp for sleeping quarters, but did not patronize our mess. As he said in his broad Yankee drawl: 'I sleep with you boys because you have lots of blankets, but I grub with the other fellows because they have better grub.' We all liked Gatling Howard. He was a congenial companion and an excellent raconteur."

On May 9th, at Clarke's Crossing, they could "hear the sound of the guns and were keen to be in it." Next day they arrived at Batoche where the decisive three-day battle was underway. Here the Corps joined Middleton's forces camped in what the General called a "zariba", a stockade of wagons "pitched on high ground in a ploughed field, surrounded by walls built of clay and sods."

Within minutes of "taking up quarters two of our horses were hit.... Less than a half a mile westward, in clear view, was the Roman Catholic Mission Church which flew a white flag and was supposed to be a refuge for women and children, but it seemed likely that it was also used as a vantage post for sniping and that it was from this point our horses had been wounded."

Middleton's battle tactics were to make "sorties... towards the village... about a mile distant, and each day ground was gained and given up again at sundown... generally resulting in killed or wounded as our men fell back with the sun in their faces. This went on for several days and all were in a fever for a general advance."

Gatling Howard was apparently also chafing under "this lack of definite results" and Wheeler used to tell a story about the frustrated Captain. "One day he approached the General in his free and easy Yankee way and said: 'Say General, do you want to let me take that thar village?' The General smiled and replied, 'I should be most happy.' 'All right, General' I want first to put my Gatling in the tower of the Church over thar.' 'No!' said the General,

'You can't do that; it's under the white flag.' 'All right then, General, take it yourself.'"

Batoche was situated on a patch of elevated prairie, above the steep banks of the Saskatchewan River valley. On May 10th, a Sunday afternoon, Wheeler suggested that he and Louis Ord wander over and examine one of the rifle pits Middleton's men had dug near camp. Suddenly Wheeler felt a flash of pain in his arm, followed by "a sharp distant report" of rifle fire. He was wounded in the left shoulder. "Ord was lying on the ground behind and the bullet whizzed by his ear so closely that a couple of inches would have been his finish." Wheeler's "wound was a trifle and I did not want to go to hospital and so lose all the fun. The doctor was a good sport" and acceded to his wish.

But it was not all fun. Next day, the D.L.S. Corps, with Middleton's red-coated men, again swarmed over the hillside. Clearly silhouetted, they were quickly picked off by the enemy. Wheeler was in the midst of the murderous melee, helping the wounded from the field. "Suddenly someone shouted: 'Kippen's gone!'" He died instantly from a head wound—"our first and only casualty...[It] brought home to us the reality of the game we were playing."

In the crucial battle of May 12th the Corps assisted in "clearing the enemy from their rifle pits on the timbered slopes above the village". Wheeler was in the field to assist although his arm was in a sling and he couldn't use his rifle. Nearby, "Gatling Howard, well-mounted, with his gun drawn by a splendid four-horse team, was racing to the scene of the engagement and before long the r-r-r-, r-r-r- of the Gatling was added to the general commotion, doing little damage but giving fine moral support".

Momentarily leaving the scene of action, Wheeler saw General Middleton dash up to ask what all the cheering was about. The officer replied, "I think they are charging the village, sir.' 'Who the devil gave them orders to charge?'" The men, exasperated by their Commander's caution, had seized the initiative to "push home the attack."

Batoche fell that day. The casualties for the D.L.S. were: Kippen killed, Wheeler, Fawcett, and Garden wounded.

On May 19th Middleton's men made "a triumphant entry into Prince Albert" where Wheeler and some of his companions spent a few days. He received letters from home and although they were billetted in "a beastly dirty camp", the stores in the settlement were soon cleaned out of supplies and the soldiers' meals included "butter and milk. A treat? You bet!" Passing the burned ruins of Fort Carlton, they rode to Battleford where Wheeler heard that his family had been notified of his death in action. He had been very anxious because he had not received letters and parcels earlier and sent a reassuring telegram at once.

With Middleton, mounted men, infantry, Gatling Howard, and some surveyors, he joined the futile chase after Chief Big Bear. Riding as much as forty miles on some days, they plunged into the wilderness. Middleton's judgment was poor—Big Bear's track was entirely unsuited for the General's heavily loaded wagons.

It was here that "the D.L.S. Corps came into its own..." Pack saddles and travois were made, and in the wooded country, treacherous with muskegs, they built roads by laying brush and quickly bridged streams with poplar stringers. Of all the General's men only the surveyors had experience travelling in the North West. At Loon Lake the chase ended—the task should have been left in the capable hands of the N.W.M.P. But it took days for Middleton to arrive at this conclusion. Captain Howard fished happily but Wheeler fumed: "General's brain unable to form any plan whatever." At last, "High-Muck-a-Muck has come to a decision and we are leaving...." To Wheeler this was a *"retreat"*. In his diary he makes it clear that he considered this an ignoble act for a commanding officer: "Middleton a damned fool anyhow."

On the way back they stopped frequently to bury the bodies of Indians which lay beside the trail. At one of Big Bear's abandoned camps Wheeler found a buffalo powder horn—he felt fortunate, for Gatling Howard usually managed to pick off the prize trophies. When he wrote his reminiscent account of the Rebellion he concluded: "Added to my recollections, I now have a disabled shoulder, the Saskatchewan Medal and Clasp, an old felt hat with a red flannel band, a pair of spurs and a rusty bayonet...."

At Fort Pitt they waited again for sixteen days "doing nothing." in an old vermin-infested Indian camp. Fortunately parcels of good food arrived from home but it was "a joyful day" when they left. They were dirty, unkempt, and irritable. "Dennis acting like a damned fool about his horse...at odds with all the surveyors....No officers assisting him." Wheeler's own temper flared when he found he had been allotted a horse he considered "an old cow." But typically, by the time they reached Port Arthur, Wheeler had forgiven Dennis and they enjoyed their cribbage games.

Looking back years later, he thought the whole episode of the Rebellion "inglorious".

There was little glory—unless a measure of glory is allowed to a brave people fighting their last battle against an alien culture. Lives were unnecessarily sacrificed. But there was one fortuitous outcome. The Rebellion had been a real threat to the tenuous union of the North West with the rest of Canada. When Van Horne got the troops west in record time, Canadians realized the value of the railway. In mid-March, when Riel had established his provisional government on the Saskatchewan, the C.P.R. was menaced by bankruptcy and the Government refused to advance another loan. By the time the troops were leaving the battlefield Parliament had granted the loan to complete the line.

And for the returning veterans there was a heroes' welcome.

Chapter V

At Battleford Arthur had taken time to call on a family he had befriended on his early survey trips and his hostess had insisted on his "partaking of whisky with *ice*." At Qu'Appelle he was paid $221.50 and scrip entitling him to a piece of homestead land. Stopping over in Winnipeg, he bought "some respectable togs"; the "boys painted the town red" but he attended a civic reception, "went for a stroll and called on Mrs. Campbell and Miss Russell." This time the journey home was by C.P.R. The last spike in that section of the railway had been driven and at every stop the welcome mat was out: the "decorations were very pretty" and the crowds cheered lustily.

He arrived home July 19th, 1885 at 7 p.m.; he was early and his family was not expecting him. They were all at church. When Mrs. Wheeler heard the news she abandoned her usual stately homeward walk. Embracing her son, she "had no breath left."

He called on the Moberlys for the evening and next day there were "lots of girls and flowers at the rink" for the returning men's breakfast. The celebration continued all day and Arthur felt "everybody making too much of me." But it was all very exhilarating. The Wheeler family had an ice-cream-tennis party and dancing on the lawn, but as Muriel and Lucy Moberly were not able to be there it "was not much fun". He "ran up to their house and played two games of tennis. They thought me crazy." Muriel and Lucy "spent the evening with us and we had a very jolly time.... Put on my new Princess Louise suit for them. Walked home with Muriel and got permission to write to her."

He went back to his Ottawa job and rose early every day to write the letters. Five days after his return to Ottawa he went with friends to a picnic and the "Misses Macoun" were there. He took up his busy social life and young ladies showered him with attention. They sent him a tie and home-made candy and he obliged by writing something in their albums; he answered their letters and accepted invitations, but the love letters to Muriel continued and eventually he wrote her mother, which seems to indicate at least an informal engagement.

He took Minnie Macoun for a canoe ride on the Rideau Canal in the moonlight and saw her again at an evening tennis party. Early in September he "wrote to Muriel. Probably the last time. Tore up a lot of letters." In October he met Minnie Macoun again at a party and took her for a stroll. Mrs. Macoun invited him to a "Frolic Eve"; he refused but accepted when Minnie expressed regret. "Enjoyed self very much for a man who doesn't dance. Danced every dance!" He answered her letters, sending a solution to her question about "Cat's tails" and acknowledging her gift of toffee. The letters to Muriel became intermittent. One came from his mother and he wrote, "denying report I was engaged."

The romance with Muriel, born during the excitement of his return from battle, was finished. Separation may have been a contributing factor but it is possible that his mother play a part. Given Mrs. Wheeler's aristocratic outlook, a Moberly alliance would certainly have been very desirable. They were an old distinguished family and their church affiliation was impeccable. She may have miscalculated and urged a formal engagement. She was a very imperious woman and if she pressed the matter her equally imperious son would dig in his heels. Also, the romantic stirring for Muriel began to cool when he was introduced into the Macoun family. Just before Chistmas vacation he "spent a very pleasant evening at the Macouns." The only Christmas gifts he sent to Ottawa from Collingwood were to the Macouns and Ryleys.

It was a happy family holiday with Kathleen, Willie, twelve-year-old Hector, and Arthur's favourite sister, the nine-year-old tomboy, Josephine, enlivening festivities. He and Willie went to the woods for evergreen boughs to decorate the Church; they all went to the school concert and on Christmas Eve the house was decorated. Christmas day began with Church service after which the boys enjoyed rifle practice. The Ryleys came from Ottawa "to dine with us". In the large drawing room, still richly scented with roast turkey, spicy desserts, pine needles, candle, cigar and wood smoke, young and old played games and "broke up an enjoyable and rather rowdy evening at 12 p.m." Arthur went to his room to copy out a story to "send to Miss Macoun".

On New Year's Eve he and Kathleen called on the large and lively Hamilton clan for tea. Then, in full evening dress, "Harry, Mac boy and self went calling. Some twenty-five calls and felt prostrated. Went to roost early as stomach in terrible state. Beer, coffee, wine."

Next day with a fine flourish he entered "epitaphs in his diary. Very naughty ones. Perhaps his battle experience had influenced him.

"No. 1: Here lie I
Snug as a bug in a rug

No. 2: Here lie I
A darn sight snugger than that other bugger.

No. 1 One can't have everything as one pleases
Little Johnny's gone to Jesus.

No. 2: It can't always be as one pleases
Perhaps Johnny's gone to blazes.

No. 3 Stranger pause and drop a tear
For Wm. Jones is buried here
But if you think that that's absurd,
Why Stranger, pause and drop a _____"

Even though this was meant for his eyes alone, the young Victorian gentleman couldn't bring himself to write the—deliciously—horrid last word.

Just before he had left Ottawa, the handsome, easy-going Gatling Howard had sauntered in to visit Arthur. They had a very pleasant time and the Captain readily agreed to present him with his photograph. With paternal concern (and youthful optimism!) Arthur also asked the Captain to see brother Willie and outline the advantages of a military career. Not even the engaging Howard could succeed in that. The seventeen-year-old charmer had no intention of undertaking anything so rigorous. He would use his special gifts in more beguiling ways.

Minnie Macoun's warm and winning manner continued to attract Arthur to the Macoun home—but there were other reasons for the close relationship which developed.

It is almost certain that Arthur had heard of Professor Macoun before they met, as reports of his expeditions and outspoken opinions appeared frequently in the Ottawa newspapers. With Arthur's keen interest in the West he had undoubtedly read of the Professor's exploits in Grant's *Ocean to Ocean.*

When Arthur had visited them before Christmas, the Professor had just returned from an exciting trip on the unfinished railway in the Selkirk Mountains of British Columbia. He and his sixteen-year-old son, William, had travelled to Canmore and Banff, where they visited the famous hot springs and collected plants on Cascade, Copper, and Castle (now Eisenhower) mountains. They then proceeded to the end of track at Donald, trekked over the dreadful tote road to Stoney Creek bridge, and went on a construction train to Rogers' Pass to camp.

Ignoring the presence of numerous grizzlies in the area, they explored for a few days, fighting their way through valleys choked with tangles of underbrush, logs and down-timber. The steep slope of Mount Avalanche challenged them so they scrambled to its high crest—the last five hundred feet were so steep that Willie, who "had no nails in his boots", climbed in stocking feet. "Almost at our feet lay the immense Illecillewaet Glacier." The Professor thought they were the first to climb on this peak, but four years before, the cantankerous little American, Major Rogers, had stood there and realized that he had found the long-sought railway pass through the Selkirks.

The Professor and his son had arranged for the train to take them back to the tote road but were so engrossed with their botanizing that they missed it. The 450-foot-long Stoney Creek bridge had to be negotiated on foot. There was no parapet, just bare rails fastened to unevenly spaced ties. Clutching packs and precious plants, they concentrated on where to put their feet. More than once the 54-year-old botanist fought back the panic of dizziness which would have hurled him into the rushing torrent hundreds of feet below. "It was the most foolhardy trip I had ever taken."

Without doubt the Professor gave a vivid account of this journey, and when he found that the attractive young bachelor Minnie was so fond of had travelled in the North West, he would hold forth on the subject he "was so full of." Clearly, Macoun kindled Arthur's longing for adventure in the far West. The two men had a great deal in common: zest for a life of action, the lure of remote and untrodden places, strength of will, self-confidence. And they were both Irish. Their relationship became one of warm, lasting, mutual regard.

But a more profound and fascinating experience awaited Arthur at the Macouns. Minnie had lured him to her nest. And there he found her cooly reserved and beautiful sister. Her fragile femininity must have been most attractive to the virile young man. Arthur Wheeler fell in love.

Clara Macoun was twenty-one; dark hair softly framed a high forehead, and finely moulded features were enhanced by a delicate, fresh complexion; deep-set eyes and sensitive mouth suggested gentle laughter. But the tall, easily carried figure was regally erect—an indication of inner strength and independence.

Her mother must have been a very patient, strong, and resourceful woman. In 1872 when her husband had so impetuously agreed to cross the continent with Fleming, she was unexpectedly left to cope for eight months with four children at their Belleville home. When her husband returned he noted: "When I arrived home I found everything in order, my wife had conducted the affairs of the establishment in an efficient manner...."

Not only that, she had given birth to their youngest child, Nellie. After all the other long treks he noted curtly: "Found all well at home... My wife was by now so accustomed to running the establishment that I was never in doubt of her want of success." She really had no alternative. It is difficult to believe that anything would have deterred the dedicated botanist from pursuing his chosen career in his own way.

In the autobiography written when he was in his late eighties, he refers to his marriage to Ellen Terrill. When he was a very young teacher in a small Ontario school he saw sixteen-year-old Ellen drive by in a carriage with her father, "Simon Terrill a well-known Quaker in that district." That first glimpse "woke me up and from that time forward, I really began to learn, my mind having focussed on her and on my studies, as an accessory to the acquisition of her as a wife." Four or five years later, in 1862, "after many discussions", they were married. That accomplished, and "now having a home", he could "commence immediately" the all-important task of forming his own "collection of plants which I had desired for some years."

In 1886 he visited England and Ireland. He records with relish, that on his arrival in England he "added to my standing...because I was placed at once on the list of distinguished Canadians.... The reader can think of me in frock coat and tall hat" attending various "functions"; he seemed amazed that formal dress was so frequently seen on the streets. Returning from this triumphant tour he realized that he now had "two marriageable daughters, besides my eldest son to keep in order and look out for their establishment in life."

There was already an eager suitor for the hand of his eldest daughter, Clara. When Mrs. Wheeler was introduced to the Macoun household the ebullient Professor would certainly refer to his hobnobbing with English elite. The excitement and child-like candor with which he expressed delight in attending "functions in frock coat and tall hat" would evoke in Arthur's mother an inward shudder of distaste. With her background these manifestations of social standing were an accepted way of life and she would consider the Professor unforgiveable brash and unpolished.

She would not dream of saying anything about the vast social gulf separating the Macouns and Wheelers but her manner would clearly indicate her disapproval of an alliance between the Wheeler heir and the daughter of someone she considered to be a member of "small Irish gentry." Today this can be dismissed as snobbery, but with Josephine and Captain Wheeler it was a naturally inherited social outlook.

Her attitude probably led to a direct and painful encounter with her son; the wound the sensitive and proud Clara sustained from the subtle snub was deep and long-lasting. The Professor's reaction is less certain.

He is very explicit about the importance he attached to social acceptance. He records the fact that the Macouns were on the visitors' list at Rideau Hall and expresses the satisfaction he felt in the company of "distinguished men." But he is also very forthright about the fact that he felt he had earned that status. He had the pride of the self-made man.

One of the reasons for his zealous advocacy of development of the North West was the sight of all the millions of empty acres awaiting settlers. His father had been one of the small landowners impoverished by the great potato famine. A photograph of the young John Macoun who emigrated to Canada in 1850 with his widowed mother and brother shows a strong-featured face with disconcertingly direct, unflinching eyes.

He worked as a farm labourer for six years, decided he wanted to be a teacher, and got his certificate in three weeks. By 1860 he had attended Normal School in Toronto for a year and had a post teaching botany at Albert College, Belleville. In his subject he was entirely self-taught; he had nurtured an intense and absorbing interest in plants since boyhood.

When Albert College attained university status he became lecturer in natural history; for years he had been writing and sending specimens to Sir William Hooker, Director of world-famous Kew Gardens. He was "making a place [for himself] in the botanical world." In 1882 the family moved to Ottawa where he worked as botanist to the Geological Survey of Canada, and three years later he was "promoted to the position of Assistant Director and Naturalist to the Survey"—a position he *demanded.*

Arthur probably spoke to the Macouns about his ancestry in a casual straight-forward manner, but Mrs. Wheeler's lofty pride may have sparked the Professor's interest in his own genealogy. Or, this may have been a natural interest which stemmed from a visit to a distant relative in England. Some interesting facts were unearthed.

In the late eighteenth century a member of another branch of the Macoun family, Rev. R. Macoun, designated as his "sole heir the Ven. Paul Helsham, L.L.D., Trinity College, Dublin, Archdeacon and Vicar-General of Ossory and Rectory of Kilfane, County Kilkenny". This exalted status in the Church of England was in itself sufficient to win Mrs. Wheeler's stamp of approval. But even more astonishing, the Archdeacon was Mrs. Wheeler's grandfather! The will of another member of the Macoun family was witnessed by the brother of Sir Richard Denny Wheeler-Cuffe, another Wheeler ancestor.

She would have been mollified by these revelations but she did not hear of them until 1901. At the time of Arthur's marriage to Clara Macoun there appears to have been a decided rift between the families. The wedding was solemnized on June 6th, 1888, in St. Andrew's Presbyterian Church, Ottawa.

It was a very quiet wedding with only a brief formal announcement appearing in newspapers. Why was the wedding such a small one? Surely the

John Macoun's daughters, Clara (left) and Minnie (right).

Professor would have preferred quite the opposite. Very likely Clara's wishes prevailed. What is even more significant is the presence of only one official witness. This was definitely unusual. Why did Arthur not have a groomsman as second witness? His brother Richard Denny had probably left for California, but Willie could have participated in that capacity. It suggests that none of the Wheelers were at the wedding of their son and heir. It is sadly ironical that the sole witness was Minnie Macoun.

Over the years Mrs. Wheeler established a cordial relationship with the Professor; so much so that in 1906 he was granted the honour of giving in marriage her youngest daughter Josephine. His ingenuous delight in his achievements was really very engaging and they enjoyed each other's company in Mrs. Wheeler's last years. But the hostility was very real when Arthur's father died.

Though he had implacably defied his parents' wishes, he was a dutiful and devoted son. When he visited Collingwood in 1888 at Christmas time, his father was dying, and at twenty-eight Arthur must have been aware of the tragedy of Captain Wheeler's last years—years of deepening realization that circumstances had frustrated all his ambitions. As he sat at the bedside for hours, tenderly feeding his father bits of ice, did Arthur feel remorse for having acted against his parents' wishes? He postponed returning to Ottawa as long as possible but within weeks he received urgent summons to return. Edward Oliver Wheeler died February 28th, 1889. Arthur was now head of the family.

A few months after her father's death, plans for Bessie's wedding went ahead, and she married Lauchlan Hamilton's brother, William. Contrasting sharply with Arthur's wedding, it was a colourful ceremony which was extensively reported in several newspapers.

During the summer of 1889 Arthur and his brother Hector went on an idyllic holiday in his canoe "Clarabell", spending more than three weeks on that beautiful waterway, the Rideau Canal. There were "glorious days" of sailing and paddling on sparkling, island-studded lakes and winding channels where ancient trees clothed high banks and spread green branches over shorelines.

They arrived at the locks at Merrickville at 10:30 p.m. after a dismal day in the rain. The lockmaster was furious when Arthur promptly roused him from his bed and there was a heated exchange. Arthur was determined to camp beyond the lock and was undaunted by the adamant refusal of the master who persistently held to the rules: canoes were never allowed passage after six—it would be setting a precedent. Arthur relished the quarrel immensely and won the argument. When they returned a few weeks later he paid his respects, and with characteristic Irish charm soon had the lockmaster laughing about the incident "when a precedent had been set."

Clara had been persuaded to join them and the day she was to arrive he got the camp all ship-shape ("flag flying") and hurried to the rendezvous. There was only a letter explaining that she could not come. "Greatly disappointed by her non-arrival." She was in fact in the early stages of pregnancy. A very dejected Arthur wrote her, imploring her to come.

She agreed and on the appointed day he went to meet the train, "hardly expecting her to come. Found her ladyship waiting for me!"

How he delighted in displaying his prowess with paddle and how anxious he was that she should enjoy every moment of his pleasure trip! On hot days they bathed in cool lakes; they bought eggs and apples from neighbouring farms and picked luscious blackberries for preserves. Enormously proud, he watched her baking biscuits in their reflector, "a great success".

They had "a grand sail" on Lower Rideau Lake where Arthur was amused to "see the Yankees on Canadian waters. They row around in easy chairs with a general factotum pulling their boats and stare at you as much as to say, 'What the devil are *you* doing here.' As for speaking to you, they are too grand for that."

On April 18th, 1890, Clara gave birth to a son, Edward Oliver. Mrs. Wheeler had a grandson to carry the family tradition. Edward Oliver was Arthur and Clara's only child. He was also the only male in the Canadian branch of the Wheelers. Richard Denny and Hector never married and the hapless Willie left no progeny.

Not long after this auspicious event Arthur made the decision to leave the Department of the Interior and go into private practice in British Columbia. There were several reasons for the move. He undoubtedly needed more income during the depression of the 1890s; the future for surveys in the North West was uncertain, but there was an urgent demand for sub-division surveyors in New Westminster. Also the young couple may have felt that separation from his mother would ease a strained relationship.

And of course there was the lure of adventure in the far West. Professor Macoun had been scouring British Columbia on collecting expeditions to Revelstoke, Kamloops, Arrow Lakes, Shuswap Lakes, the Fraser and Okanagan valleys. Naturally, Arthur's sprightly father-in-law had been rhapsodic about the glories of British Columbia.

On March 11, 1891, Arthur Wheeler set out to see "the rugged magnificence" of Butler's "immense range of mountains."

Chapter VI

Travelling by train, A. O. Wheeler passed through familiar country. West of Winnipeg the straggling little townsites he had surveyed had not changed much, but widely scattered cultivated fields broke the monotony of the flat plains. Passing into what is now Alberta, he saw scattered herds of cattle peacefully grazing on the boundless acres of large ranches. He focused his attention on the western horizon.

Through soft blue haze he glimpsed patches of white; tawny foothills billowed to dark green timbered swells. Then towering above them, sharply etched against the clear blue sky, the mighty ramparts of the Rockies lifted snow-capped peaks in shining splendor.

Entering between their portals, the track turned north, the immense clay-coloured bastions of Mount Rundle appeared on the left, and straight ahead, snow glistened on the fissured pyramid of Cascade Mountain. Soon the panorama of summits filled the whole field of vision. Following the valley of the Bow River to Laggan (today's Lake Louise Station) the C.P.R.'s Imperial Limited turned west to ascend Kicking Horse Pass. The very sharp descent was made very slowly, taking forty-seven minutes to travel the eight miles to the foot of the Pass.

"On we glide in serpentine folds, down the valley of the Kicking Horse, now with a roar into the darkness of a tunnel; now overhanging white boiling waters with the rush and swirl of the river always in our ears, first on one side and then on the other. Above, an endless array of crags and rocks rise forever; while the hoarse, weird shriek of the train's whistle adds the last touch, and reverberating in every crack and hollow intensifies the fantasy of it all. It is with a sigh, akin to relief, that the tension is broken and the gorge opens upon the dark green, more gentle landscape of the Columbia Valley."

The train crawled up the eastern slope of the Selkirks "on a patch carved directly from the mountain side"; it toiled to the summit of Rogers' Pass and down the grade where uplifted crags guarded the deep, sharp-cut valley clothed in its cool, dense forest of spruce and giant cedars. Halting at Rogers' Pass station near Glacier House, the Transcontinental disgorged all passengers who "gazed in awe and wonder" at the Illecillewaet Glacier, a "wildly broken cascade of ice falling three thousand feet from the skyline into the primeval forest below." Spectacular scenery on the rest of the journey to the Pacific "held the fancy always on the *qui vive*" but none surpassed the vivid impressions of the Rockies and Selkirks.

Travelling through the canyon of the Fraser River, he must have marvelled at the courage and tenacity of the men who surveyed and laid the track through the fearful, constricted cleft of those rocky walls. After its final lash of fury the mighty Fraser flowed gently at sea level where its many-fingered delta merged with the Pacific.

Arthur, Clara, and baby Oliver settled with their maid into a house on Armstrong Street in the thriving community of New Westminster. With a population of over six thousand, it offered the amenities of churches, hospital, public library, newspaper, Y.W.C.A., opera house, schools, and three public parks.

On weekends, families thronged aboard the steamer "Lillooet"; with buntings gaily fluttering, it took young and old on picnic excursions up the Fraser River. When Arthur was not in the field he and Clara could enjoy these picnics or watch cricket and lacrosse matches at Queen's Park. There, too, they participated in the famous May Day festivities. This was a day for the children with the distribution of "sweets, nuts and oranges", the colourful May Pole Dance and parade, when the chosen queen for the day rode in her decorated carriage, accompanied by marching bands. In winter adults and children skated on Burnaby Lake and the New Year was ushered in with fireworks, band concerts, the midnight tolling of all the town's bells, and church services.

The "Royal City Debating Club" met for "Conversations and smoking concerts". This all-male group invited the Women's Christiam Temperance Union as special guests when they debated whether or not the franchise should be extended to women. Surprisingly, the affirmative side won.

There were, of course, the balls in the Opera House and Willie Wheeler's presence undoubtedly enhanced these occasions. Unfortunately, such agreeable diversions failed to compensate for the fact that Arthur was determined to make his debonair bachelor brother earn a living as a member of the survey team.

Wheeler's private survey contracts were augmented by work he did on timber berths for the Department of the Interior. He sent a report of a mining location north of Kamloops to the Department in the spring of 1891 and also one of a survey of Tree Island in the Fraser River in 1892. That summer he completed work on timber berths on the east side of the Columbia River south of Revelstoke and Salmon Arm in the Shuswap Lake area. This work also took him into the Stave and Pitt Rivers which rise in the mountains of today's Garibaldi Park. He was being initiated into the difficulties of running lines in British Columbia's forests and learning the treacherous ways of her rivers. It was on the Pitt River survey that Willie enjoyed a brief moment of glory.

Whenever the Wheeler sons were discussed by family and friends, Arthur was always referred to as "the perfect gentleman", Richard Denny was "the nicest", and the youngest was "poor Hector" because of his quiet courage in the face of poor health and infirmity. But mention of Willie evoked a shrug of resignation or exasperation. He was a handsome n'er-do-well and no one worried unduly about this—for generations Wheelers had supported carefree younger sons. However, during the next few years Arthur attempted to instill in him some sense of responsibility.

When the work at Pitt Lake was complete they descended the River; the canoe carrying their supplies, instruments, and Arthur's jacket containing the field notebooks was in the charge of two crack paddlers. Somehow the French Canadian in the stern got his signals crossed with the Scot in the bow and in a flash the canoe overturned. The paddlers snatched a snagged tree and were righting their canoe, but Arthur leapt into the river to rescue the jacket and precious notebooks. The current instantly swept him off his feet. Willie grabbed him by the scruff of the neck, yelling, "Come back, you damned fool! Do you want to drown?" Family opinion was unanimous: it was the only time Willie had ever done a useful turn.

Without the notebooks Arthur and his men had to return to the field for three weeks and do the work all over again.

In the early nineties British Columbia's mining development proceeded at a feverish pace; railways were being pushed into the interior valleys, and in Vancouver there was a land boom which crashed in 1893. Mortgages were being foreclosed and the unemployed lined up at soup kitchens.

By 1892 Wheeler was applying for more work in the North West. Characteristically, he appealed to friends who were Members of Parliament for recommendations. "Hugh J. Macdonald Esq." wrote at his request to the Deputy Minister of the Interior, remarking that "Wheeler is, I believe, a very competent man..." and J. S. Dennis, Chief Inspector of Surveys, wrote that "his surveys have been well and honestly performed, the lines being straight and well opened out in timber and brush and the corners properly marked."

In that season he was successful in getting a contract for township outlines and subdivisions near Willingdon in what is now Alberta. The C.P.R. had built a branch line from Calgary to Edmonton; in 1893 surveys for settlers and townsites were required and Wheeler surveyed in the rich parkland between these two major centres.

Professor Macoun spent that summer collecting on Vancouver Island and Mrs. Macoun and their youngest daughter, Nellie, came to stay with Clara. The family reunion was a happy one. When Arthur decided that his future would be more secure in the civil service, Clara was undoubtedly very pleased at the prospect of moving back to Ottawa. In January, 1894, the Minister of the Interior had approved Wheeler's application for appointment to the Topographical Survey Branch.

Colonel J. S. Dennis, who had been Wheeler's commanding officer during the Riel Rebellion, had just returned from a tour of the western United States where he had examined irrigation practices. He was convinced that intensive surveys to determine the extent and feasibility of irrigation in what is now southern Alberta and Saskatchewan were imminent. Working under Dennis, Wheeler took a survey crew into the area in June 1894, the year that large-scale irrigation was introduced in western Canada.

For years the great pioneer surveyor, William Pearce of Calgary, had urged the Dominion government to act on his enthusiastic recommendations that irrigation would transform immense tracts of land into fertile farms. When Mormons from Utah settled in the Cardston area and irrigated their land, Pearce's convictions were confirmed. Several private companies were formed to promote and extend irrigation, and after visiting Calgary in 1892, the Minister of the Interior, T. N. Daly, realized that a complete topographical survey must be made to prepare for irrigation.

Professor Macoun was also dispatched to the south-western plains that year. When he had visited the prairies in 1879 he "fearlessly announced that the so-called arid country was one of unsurpassed fertility." His appraisal, which influenced the C.P.R.'s change of route, flatly contradicted the previous report of Palliser, the dashing Irish explorer who had stated that the area was one of very light rainfall and was in fact an extension of the Great American Desert. Palliser saw the region during an interval of drought—Macoun first saw it in one of its wet seasons. However, by 1893, many of the farmers who had taken up homesteads bordering the railway were abandoning their land because recurring drought spelled disaster.

For six years Wheeler surveyed south of Calgary along Jumpingpound Creek, Elbow River, Fish Creek, the Sheep and Highwood Rivers, Willow Creek, Oldman River, Pincher Creek, Waterton, Little Bow, Belly, St. Marys, and Milk Rivers which flow through the light rainfall region of the western plains. Initially he was instructed to transmit a general idea of the hydrography and topography, but each year his work increased in detail and precision. Fixing measuring instruments to determine the rate of flow and discharge of these waterways, his party traced them to their headwaters in the high foothills and eastern range of the Rockies. Reports on timber resources, fire destruction and existing trails were recorded; suitable sites for reservoirs were located and surveyed. The area was mapped.

During his irrigation surveys Wheeler occupied almost two hundred stations, exposing hundreds of plates. When field work was finished he developed and enlarged the photos to compile his maps.

Outfitting in Calgary with a buckboard, three carts and seven horses, he and seven or eight men, including teamsters and a cook, made what was then a long journey from the centre of Calgary to the top of the benchlands where the city's south-west suburbs sprawl today. The unfolding vista was one of incomparable splendour.

Under the wide sky the unbounded plain stretched to the rim of the eastern horizon; ahead lay billowing foothills, their grass-cover the colour and texture of gopher pelts; steep-sided coulees meandered in curves, their soft folds clustered with green aspen or crested with evergreens. And in the west huge slabs of the earth thrust upward—the Rockies, guarding the prairies.

This was the country where they worked and lived for five or six months of the year. It was virtually empty. They often travelled for days or camped for weeks without encountering another human being.

During each of the first three seasons the party worked as far south as the Milk River. In the spring, rivers and streams heading in the mountains became torrents and fording them was no easy matter. Axles and wheels on the buckboard snapped and everything had to be portaged across many a stream, and a man sent to the nearest village for replacements. On summer days heat waves shimmered over sage-grey bunch grass—everything was parched, dessicated, and grasshoppers zithered among the cacti. Ominous billows of smoke seethed and blotted out the sun, and with incredible speed the wind-driven flames of the prairie fire licked up tinder-dry grass. To save their

A. O. Wheeler's camp southwest of Calgary.

camps they fought the fires, but nothing could be done about the lingering smoke which maddeningly delayed photographic work.

Weather in the high foothills was unpredictable. Often instruments were packed up to suitable ridges in fine weather and on their arrival clouds would descend. In mid-October 1898 a high camp was set up in the snow because conditions were ideal. Wheeler had just taken "a few views" when heavy wet snow swirled from suddenly leaden skies. Determined to finish his work, he stayed at the high camp overnight, but for twenty-four hours the wind raged, nearly blowing his tent away. Lighting a fire was out of the question, so he could only stay between his blankets. Next day was clear and he hurried to begin his camera work. The wind blew "a gale" and a piece of the tripod blew away, the thermometer was smashed, and the precious camera was in jeopardy. After three days of unabated winds he had to retreat for the season.

He learned to tolerate these frustrations though he was always impatient with anything which impeded effective action. He was less tolerant of delays due to human irresponsibility. The crew member who was sent for mail and supplies but "went on a bender" instead, losing both mail and goods, was subjected to a fiery eruption of rage from his chief. The cook was more prudent. He just left without warning.

Prolonged isolation was often cause for these defections. Wheeler, a very sociable man, often felt the need for varied companionship, especially a feminine presence. When camped near Indian reserves he rode to visit the agent and his wife after work. Riding back to camp on one occasion, he saw the setting sun sink below the peak-rimmed horizon; briefly, sky and mountains were bathed in gold; slowly the jagged outline of distant peaks shaded to black against a background merging mother-of-pearl rose with soft yellow and pale aqua. The splendour filled him with a deep sense of peace and contentment.

As field work always continued until mid-October or later, the long buckboard journey to Calgary was frequently made in snowstorms. As party leader, Arthur often travelled the last stages by train. Willie, as assistant, was left to bring in the outfit. Jolting over frozen trails and camping on open prairie were no delight for Arthur's brother.

In a letter to his mother several years later, Arthur remarked ". . . there are some very comical things about Bill, one of which is his extreme dislike of being uncomfortable." This appraisal was intended to comfort his aging mother. Privately he probably found his traits less endearing.

Spending the winter in their Ottawa home, Wheeler compiled his reports of the season's work and did the painstaking work of map-making from data collected. He usually travelled to Collingwood for a short visit where Willie, Hector, and occasionally Kathleen continued to live for a few more years. These were happy days with much calling on old friends for "evening games of whist and crochinole", teas and dinners. Mrs. Wheeler and Josephine had taken over Clara and Arthur's cottage in Ottawa when they had gone to New Westminster. Minnie Macoun was now married and living in Boston where Clara visited with Oliver when Arthur was in the field. The Professor or Mrs. Macoun always met Arthur's train in the fall, often bringing Oliver. And pleasant evenings were spent with Clara at home or at the theatre and frequently he went with the Professor to "mother's and played halma."

In April of 1896 Conservative Sir Charles Tupper became Prime Minister. He was distantly related to the Wheelers, being a member of a Tupper branch of the family which emigrated to Canada. Under an entail created by Captain Edward Wheeler's cousin, Sir Charles Frederick Denny Wheeler-Cuffe, the Wheeler estates passed, on the extinction of the male line of the Wheeler-Cuffes, to the descendants of his sister, who had married a Tupper so that the Tuppers now own Lyrath House and estates. Arthur may not have been aware of the relationship but his mother, with her keen eye for genealogy, probably was.

In any event, Arthur, being a staunch Conservative, undoubtedly took a lively interest in the election as the local candidate in what is now Alberta, was a very good friend, the Honourable T. B. H. Cochrane. They were also related, Cochrane being a brother of Mrs. Wheeler's friend and relative, Lady Minnie Cochrane, who was Lady-in-Waiting to Queen Victoria's daughter. The Cochranes had taken up thousands of acres of grazing land near High River. Subsequently they developed a sheep ranch, a small wool industry, and a saw mill at the village of Mitford, named after Lady Cochrane's relatives.

It is not likely that Arthur was present at the June election rally which made headlines in a Calgary newspaper. Cochrane may not have been either, but according to the press it was "A Successful Smoker" attended by "a very enthusiastic and happy lot of Conservatives." There was musical entertainment, "cigars, liquid and edible refreshments were handed around and partaken of...[and] a number of other very interesting features were introduced during the evening." This delightfully enigmatic statement leads to intriguing speculation as to the nature of those "interesting features". When the party broke up in the small hours, Calgary's most respected gentlemen "lined up in the street in front of the building and time and again gave three cheers for candidate Cochrane in a most lusty manner which could be heard a mile away"!

Cochrane was defeated by Liberal Frank Oliver of Edmonton, with whom Arthur would lock horns fifteen years later, and Tupper was succeeded by Laurier.

Early in the 1897 season, smoke still hampered photographic work but in mid-June the long drought broke with dramatic suddenness. Four days of torrential rain in the mountains turned quiet streams into raging torrents; bridges were swept away, farm buildings overturned, and the countryside flooded. Wheeler, who was camped near Jumpingpound Creek, ferried farmers and families to safety in his canvas boat.

In Calgary trains were delayed for days; houses on the flats were swept away and visiting Indians daringly swam their ponies into the swirling water to help with rescue work. Calgary's saloons were busy as well. Thirsty cowboys in from the round-up relieved parched throats and the prestigious Alberta Hotel bar was crammed with eminent patrons—the water was too muddy to drink so the substituted libations were justified.

Professor Macoun joined Arthur at the Jumpingpound camp to botanize as soon as weather permitted. As usual, the Professor preceded the party but arrangements were made for a rendezvous that evening. Making his way over flooded country, he arrived at the ranch which he understood to be the meeting place. The owner was just leaving, but he made him welcome and Macoun "got some victuals", hung his clay-dripping clothes to dry and made himself comfortable in the rancher's bed.

When his host returned he announced that he had just come from Wheeler's camp and all the men were highly concerned about the Professor—they had been out looking for him all afternoon. Wheeler arrived after a tiring journey and was greatly relieved to find his father-in-law, who was "glad we were all together again and I decided that I would not be advance man again for the season." A photograph of him at Wheeler's camp shows the 66-year-old botanist in battered clothes with his eyes twinkling merrily under bushy brows. He was as happy as the little rock rabbit who also collects grass all summer.

It was not the first time he had been lost. In 1875, making his way from the Peace River country to Fort Carlton with an old Indian, he sat down to rest beside the trail and read a few pages of *The Heart of Midlothian*. He then strode on to overtake his companion but became frightened when he couldn't find him; he felt he had been left to fend for himself a hundred miles from the nearest outpost. He turned back to see if there was any sign of the cart and the Indian leaving the trail, but found none: "He had just disappeared!" Suddenly he noticed a dead horse beside the road, just like the one he had seen earlier, except it was on the left side of the road instead of the right. The light dawned: "I'd been all day going back on the road I had come...the scales immediately fell from my eyes...and I discovered that instead of sitting on the right side of the road, I had sat on the left, and on arising I turned back instead of forward." When the Indian came searching for him the Professor

Professor John Macoun in camp southwest of Calgary.

explained all of this. But the explanation was too complex and Macoun was much put out when the Indian insisted on telling everyone he had been *ill* "when in reality I had been lost."

The wet season of 1897 made travel extremely difficult for the packtrains Wheeler used in high country but it provided excellent conditions for photography. He was now in charge of the Irrigation Surveys and directed the work of two other crews in the field. His youngest brother, Hector, began working as his assistant. He lacked the dashing charm of his brothers but was a very patient, kind, gentle, and unselfish man. He had apprenticed for five years as an engraver with the British American Bank Note Company, and under his brother's supervision he qualified as one of the most skilful topographical draughtsmen in Canada; many of Wheeler's beautiful early maps were the product of Hector's gifted pen.

In June of 1897 the British Empire celebrated the diamond jubilee of Queen Victoria's reign. The occasion was not ignored by A. O. Wheeler even though he was in the field with a handful of men. He declared a holiday, ran up the flag and organized "shooting and cricket matches, sprints and a smoking concert. Had a very jolly day."

Calgary's official celebration was less spirited. For days the paper filled columns with reports of the great events city fathers were organizing. Expectant citizens crowded the main street, awaiting the promised fireworks and parades. They never materialized. With splendid improvisation, dependable "Cappy" Smart, the colourful fire chief and leader of the Fire Brigade Band, stepped into the breach and marched his uniformed musicians back and forth before the assembled throng; the band's director, E. Crispin Smith added a touch of colour in his bearskin busby, long Prince Albert coat with white belt and sash. But the editor lamented next day that disappointed Calgarians had "not had a proper opportunity to display the loyal and patriotic sentiments that swelled in their breasts on this auspicious day."

The depression ended in 1898 and the West was booming. The tidal wave of immigration was rising; mining in the East Kootenay district of British Columbia (which would soon have rail connections with Calgary) was flourishing. Straggling groups of men in search of wealth trekked through Calgary on their way to the Klondike gold fields. The town would benefit from all these developments, and Arthur Wheeler decided to make his home there.

As soon as he returned from the East in May, he bought a lot and sent Clara the plans for the cottage he was going to have built. Late in September, while carpenters and plumbers were still putting finishing touches to the house, Clara and Oliver arrived.

Calgary around the turn of the century was confined to less than a square mile of business and residential streets in what is the central core of today's metropolis. Clara and Arthur's house stood on the site of today's Summit Hotel; from its fashionable bow windows in the living and dining room they could see the Bow River and the bare tawny uplands which surrounded the town, and nearly all of the business section was within sight of their large garden.

Beside false-fronted wooden stores stood substantial sandstone buildings: the famous Alberta Hotel with the longest bar west of Winnipeg, the Hudson's Bay store, Bank of Montreal, and the C.P.R. station with its beautifully landscaped gardens and dining room where the company's hostess, Mrs.

Bowden, rang a bell from the verandah promptly at noon, calling businessmen to come to a good dinner for thirty-five cents. Ladies lifted long graceful skirts above their ankles to escape the mud at street crossings and booted cowboys' footsteps rang on plank sidewalks. Where Eaton's store stands today there was an open field, colourful with Indian teepees. There, on the back streets, were the necessary livery barns, blacksmith shops, feed stores, and the pungent aroma of ammonia and manure mixed with the clean air blowing from the mountains.

A very large segment of the population was British and many were "gentry"; recreational and social life reflected this. At Elbow Park, Clara and Arthur watched polo matches; at the "Cochrane Ranche", even in blinding dust storms, croquet balls clicked; they could watch cricket, "that fine manly sport of our English fathers" (as the editor of the *Herald* proclaimed), or they could go in a surrey to watch the Calgary Turf Club's steeple chase.

In a very short time the Wheelers were enjoying a congenial social life with friends who were predominantly members of the Anglican Church of the Redeemder. Dean Paget and his wife joined the Cochranes, the Bell-Irvings, and bank managers Rowley and Wilgress as the Wheelers' friends. With them they attended the gala occasions which were the highlight of the winter social scene: the Fire Brigade Ball and Hospital Ball held in Hull's Opera House, a large arena-like building, and the Winter Skating Carnival with its fancy costume parade at Victoria Rink. There was a lively interest in drama with local actors staging plays and these were augmented by the professional touring companies so popular at the time. Occasionally there were exhibitions to astonish residents.

In 1896, in an old feed store, "Edison's Kinetoscope" could be seen. "Do not fail to see the latest invention" the advertisement urged, for it was "to the eye what the phonograph is to the ear, reproducing living movements so that spectators will find it hard to assure themselves that they are not looking at the actual scene from life...."

And of course Clara and Arthur entertained in their pleasant home. With its fireplace, good furniture, and an abundance of photographs, dresser scarves, cushions and typical Victorian accessories, it had a comfortable atmosphere. On bright crisp days, he and Clara would hire a cutter with a prancing horse and bundle up in furs and a snug lap robe to "enjoy that rare treat in the West, a sleigh ride" to Crescent Heights or as far out as the Sarcee Indian Reserve. In summer they could stroll up Mission Hill where Clara could delight in the profusion of wild roses, clematis, honeysuckle, and violets which carpeted the ground.

When he returned to the field in the spring of 1899, he took Clara and Oliver along as far as the Bell-Irving's ranch where they spent a month while Arthur worked. Clara's youngest sister, Nellie, came West for an extended visit. As his administrative work now required more frequent visits from the field to the Calgary office, he was able to enjoy week-end picnics with friends. These were restful and casual affairs with lunches eaten beneath great balm-of-Gileads beside a stream. But there was nothing casual about the clothing worn. Arthur and happy young Oliver wore stout woollen breeches with white shirts, ties and tweed caps; Nellie, Clara, and a very coquettish Miss Sally Bell-Irving wore heavy flared woollen skirts, belts, sheer blouses with leg-o-mutton sleeves, mannish ties, and trim flat-crowned straw sailor hats.

*A picnic west of Calgary. Behind young Oliver
Wheeler (from left to right), Miss Bell-Irving,
Clara Wheeler and Nellie Macoun.*

Serving a thriving ranching community, Calgary had already acquired
its distinctive character as "Cowtown". Prominent visitors were inevitably
treated to specially arranged programs at the race track and driven to the
more prosperous ranchers' homes for western hospitality. It must have been
exciting for Oliver to see for the first time the exhibition featuring Indian
pony races, broncho busting, and steer roping.

But that year when he accompanied his father to the field he saw the
actual round-ups. The country beside the Bow south-west of Calgary was
awesomely empty. Here and there a ranch with its buildings surrounded by
rail fences of poplar poles made an island of human habitation. And in spring,
groups of twenty or thirty cowboys with up to sixty horses skilfully rode herd
on milling, bawling cattle.

With his father's party, nine-year-old Oliver made sharp descents into narrow valleys where mountain streams rushed over treacherously wet boulders. He learned to ford them on horseback. In pouring rain, father and son climbed a high ridge to photograph; they waited out a storm in the high camp. And in September, again at a high camp, they were buffetted by wind, hail, and snow. Oliver was taken to the train to return to school, but Wheeler continued field work until mid-November.

Early the next year he received instructions to close the Calgary office. That season he completed his irrigation surveys which provided indispensable information for the expansion of irrigation in southern Alberta. Professor Macoun must have been delighted that his son-in-law was instrumental in fulfilling his daring prophecy that the area would some day be the "Garden of the West".

During the summer of 1900 Wheeler did a photo-topographical survey of the Crowsnest Pass mining area. He and Hector occupied higher camera stations and for the first time Arthur's diary notes: "Got very nearly played out going up the mountain." Again Oliver was climbing with his father.

In February of 1901 Clara and Oliver left for Ottawa where she would remain with her parents while Oliver settled into school at Trinity College, Port Hope. Arthur and Hector finished the Crowsnest mapping and waited for word about the next assignment from the Department of the Interior.

In the interval he "had the boys in for chess until 2 a.m.," made social calls and dined with friends; jauntily sporting "a button-hole", he took Mrs. Wilgress to church and Miss Bell-Irving to the ball at Alexandra Hall. On April 29th the Surveyor General's instructions arrived.

What can be said about the character of the man, who in the prime of life at forty-one was going to embark on the most challenging and rewarding years of his life?

Dynamic, strong-willed, with a volatile temperament, he was a man of his time with a Victorian sense of duty and dedication. Imperious? Decidedly. A long inheritance had conferred on him an air of command—a natural "presence". He was never plagued by the modern search for an identity. Twenty years spent on Canada's western frontier had softened some of his inborn attitudes of class distinction; though he may have preferred the friendship of his social equals, he worked with and enjoyed the company of all manner of men. Vain? Arrogant? He was humble only in the presence of "the Great Hills".

Chapter VII

Wheeler cherished memories of his railway journeys through the mountains; especially vivid were those of the Rogers Pass section where the rails snake their way through the Selkirk Range. "It was, therefore, with a thrill of satisfaction I realized on reading my instructions, that my work lay among the biggest of the big fellows, and that I was to go into the heart of the Selkirks."

During construction, the C.P.R.'s dynamic Van Horne, making an inspection tour, had recognized the potential value of the rugged alpine grandeur traversed by the line: "We can't export the scenery, so we'll import the tourists." To avoid the heavy cost of hauling dining cars across the steepest grades, he had small chalets built; the first one, Glacier House, opened in 1886. It nestled in a recess at the base of Mount Abbot in the twilight shades of a semi-tropical forest; directly opposite, a white-cascade dropped 1200 feet from Eagle Peak; the Illecillewaet Glacier better known then as the Great Glacier, and the sharp rock monolith of Mount Sir Donald formed a fitting climax for a beautifully impressive backdrop.

Within a few years Glacier House was filled to capacity with travellers from all over the world and the close proximity of splendid peaks and glaciers acted as a magnet for American and European mountaineers. Exploiting this attraction, the C.P.R. brought Swiss guides to assist aspiring climbers and in 1901 it persuaded the great Edward Whymper to spend the season in the Rockies. "The Lion of the Matterhorn" would make headlines.

Surveyor General Deville had already initiated a photo-topographic survey in the railway belt of the Rockies and had intended to continue the work in 1901. But on hearing of Whymper's visit, he decided on the Selkirk survey instead in order to give the world-famous Whymper a clear field. Apparently the C.P.R. assumed that he would not only accomplish prodigious first ascents but also present them with maps. Whymper's plans were not so ambitious, as Wheeler discovered, when, by a fortuitous coincidence, he met the "Prince of Mountaineers" on the train to Banff.

Wheeler was going to do a reconnaissance of the terrain to be mapped and recognized Whymper as his fellow-passenger. With characteristic poise, he introduced himself. It is indicative of his courtesy and presence that he was not rebuffed—Whymper, whose features were as sharply chiselled as the crags he conquered, was renowned for his imperious and arrogant attitude toward lesser mortals. As they were both stopping off at the Banff Springs Hotel, Whymper even invited him to inspect his alpine equipment. Wheeler was very excited about the meeting and wrote Clara about it immediately.

Mrs. Bell-Irving was camping in Banff and he had arranged to spend the day sightseeing with her; they took the path to Bow Falls and climbed Tunnel Mountain. His diary notes: "Enjoyed day immensely. So did Fritz." Fritz was his beloved black Irish Setter who was his companion on almost every climb. Another entry is terse: "Went to museum as arranged with curator. Couldn't get in as he was *Hors du Combat.*"

Boarding the train again on a glorious spring morning, he was enchanted by the passing scenery. "The sun shone in dazzling splendour on snowy peaks and the fleecy clouds cast moving shadows on the ever-changing landscape....The mind climbed rapidly through cool dark forests of pine, up ragged rock precipices, across shining snow-fields and glistening glaciers, occupying peak after peak and gazing afar on the silent grand array....With a shock, the mind returns to realities and wonders how in creation survey instruments, cameras and the necessities of existence are ever to be taken up to these outposts of earth."

For ten days, starting at Revelstoke, he inspected the country eastward along the railway as far as Beavermouth, most of it on foot. At the end of one humid, sweltering day: "It was with a feeling of thankfulness that we saw the red section house at Albert Canyon; twenty-two miles of railway ties become tiring even though surrounded by the most glorious scenery in the world."

Earlier, he and two railway employees accompanying him, were crossing "a long wooden trestle...; midway across a freight train suddenly emerged from a cutting at the other end and took the trestle. There was nothing for it but to hang on to the side timbers of the bridge as best we might, not a comfortable position with a pack on your back and a hundred-foot drop" to the cataract below. "That was the longest and slowest train I ever saw...."

Mrs. Young, "the charming and efficient hostess" at Glacier House, placed at his disposal the C.P.R. Swiss guides. He realized that he needed professional climbing instruction for work on high ice and snow fields. "I shall not readily forget my first climb...accompanied by six of them, all keen to impart information....We parted with mutual respect and esteem...." This is only partly true. Some of the guides did indeed become life-long friends, but they were very proud of their skill and experience and were not pleased when Wheeler airily dismissed them, deciding he could manage on his own after the briefest professional help. Although he used them occasionally, "finding them careful, patient workers and cheerful companions", by the end of the season he felt that he and his men were "quite their equals" on rock climbs. In an improving state of mind he remarked too, that these stolid fellows in rather shapeless tweeds would benefit from "a more careful attention to the details of costume...to fill more nearly the prevailing idea of the hardy and picturesque Swiss mountaineer."

On the first climb it was a stimulating experience to see the panorama of peaks which would challenge him during the coming weeks. There was also the "added charm...of climbing on snow...and the exhilaration and excitement of setting foot upon a glacier for the first time. All was new and interesting...."

Back in Calgary he hired men. At Golden, pack horses were bought and shipped to Albert Canyon station, and on July 5th the survey began.

"We were deeply involved in the mysteries of the diamond hitch and already had several of the ponies loaded, when along came the delayed train, puffing, panting, full of business and its own importance. Pack animals are always restless for some time after the loads are cinched on, and the train rushing in beside them settled the matter. A general stampede ensued; ponies careened in every direction, prancing and snorting; men rushed here and there, shouting and swearing, trying to hold them; everything was frantic and desperate. Despite our efforts, one broke away, dashed madly through the brush and fallen timber, leaped a tree trunk four feet high, and rolled head over heels on the other side; then, having burst the hook from the lash-rope and scattered the pack to the four winds, went wildly scouring through the clearing.... The train was crowded with passengers by the latest steamer from Japan, and the observation car full of people. They cheered, clapped their hands and waved, while some even went the length of shouting 'Encore!' They were evidently under the impression that it was all arranged by the fatherly arrangment of the C.P.R. for their amusement.

The first stations occupied were less than eight thousand feet high, allowing the party to become acclimatized. Even these, however, were not reached without hardship. Many years later Wheeler wrote of the Selkirks: "These wonderful regions are guarded by dense forests...almost impassable thickets of downward-pointing alder, bracken, Devil's Club....Devil's Club. What an experience is Devil's Club! Imagine a bare stick an inch thick and five or eight feet high with a spread of tropical-looking palmated leaves, set off with a bunch of bright red berries. The entire surface of the stick is covered by sharp, fine spines and the canes grow so close together that sometimes it is impossible to force a way through them without using an axe. The points of the spines break off in the flesh, causing it to fester and become very painful."

However, these "difficulties add zest to the endeavour to reach the bright uplands; and there is always what lies beyond the skyline as a final goal.... The glorious heights, the white, shining snowfields and the innumerable crystal ice-falls always make me think of them as the Dear, Delightful, Devilish Selkirks."

Because the season was short and there were few days suitable for photographic work, Wheeler set a strenuous and backbreaking pace. Within a few months he was an accomplished mountaineer, but even with his extraordinary physical stamina, after frequent soakings in dripping underbrush he notes, "Rheumatism very bad. Consulted Dr. Schaeffer about pains in my chest."

"An ascent with packs usually takes from five to six hours, the work at a summit, three to four hours, according to the number of camera stations, and the descent about three hours, or twelve hours' continuous labour of the hardest kind; for the instrumental work requires the closest attention and it is quite as fatiguing as the physical portion.... Try this sort of thing for five or six days in the week and then see how you feel on the seventh."

Naturally gregarious, Wheeler's genial manner won the ready cooperation of all the C.P.R. staff from the management to "the humblest employees of

52

Mount Sir Donald and the Illecillewaet Glacier in the Selkirk Mountains.

the line." On one occasion, using a Company hand car to move camp, he and his men were assured that the line would be clear for at least two hours, and they entered a snowshed. Half way through they saw "a man silhouetted against the opening at the farther end; frantically waving his arms, his meaning was clear: something was coming down the line. To stop the car on the up-grade, jump off and lift it from the rail was the work of a few seconds; then we found to our horror that there was not room between the track and the side of the shed. At this moment an engine from Rogers' Pass entered with a blood-curdling whistle. We were still struggling with the car as the engine stopped, thirty feet away. Fortunately, it was a light engine...had there been a heavy train behind—well, something would have been smashed."

Of the thirty-five camera stations occupied before the season ended in late October, two were over ten thousand feet, and on these Swiss guides accompanied Wheeler and his assistant. He did this reluctantly, and only because there was no time to waste in choosing the best routes. The highest peak climbed was the dominant Mount Sir Donald at 10,808 feet. They started for its summit at 2 a.m. in moonlight and returned to camp at ten o'clock in the evening.

On another occasion, in 1902, darkness overtook them two thousand feet above camp and they "could only feel [their] way down....Twice, climbing through cedar scrub, I felt my body swinging in empty space." He concluded that "climbing lacks much of its charm in the night time".

After a climb the same year, they had to pitch camp in the dark on a trail barely two feet wide; with ice axes they dug wide shelves from the mountain side, rolled up in blankets and slept. It was "rather eerie" to realize that they were protected from a fall over the precipice by stakes driven in beside their improvised beds, but nonetheless, "there was much merriment over the situation" next morning.

Often "the Devilish Selkirks" were wrapped in a damp shroud and "all was grim, black and wet." They crossed the Asulkan névé when it was "buried in a thick bank of clouds; five yards in every direction was a blank white wall...it was a case of prod with the ice axe, take a step and prod again," feeling for the snow-covered crevasses which gashed the ice.

Two young apprentice-surveyors who had been with him on the Crowsnest survey left, unwilling to work under such hazardous conditions—and such a demanding chief. Wheeler had replaced them with two Englishmen from Revelstoke. As they were crossing the Asulkan in the clouds, one man plummetted up to his neck in a crevasse. "'Hello, I'm in a crevasse,' he called. 'Indeed, sir,' replied his companion earnestly, 'it *was* clever of you to find it!'" Both men also sought less strenuous work shortly.

In the second season of the work Wheeler was occupying ever higher peaks—three of them over eleven thousand feet. Twelve-year-old Oliver climbed with his father and ascended a peak 8,379 feet high; as there was no evidence of a previous ascent (at least, "by anyone of that age"), Wheeler christened it Mount Oliver. Another mountain, 11,023 feet high, was a first ascent and he was not at all modest about naming it Mount Wheeler. Swiss guides were still employed for the higher climbs, but by the end of the 1902 season Wheeler was obviously delighted with his mastery of climbing techniques. On Mount Purity he differed with them about the route of descent and recorded with relish that his route brought him down fifteen minutes before his guides.

Wheeler's Irish setter, Fritz, who had gained a reputation as a mountain climber, was happily following the party one day to a high station above Geikie Glacier. The men had some difficulty negotiating a steep rock face; Fritz, sensing their tension, became excited and "sprang from the rock, slipped and fell seven hundred feet to a ledge." He was dead when he stopped rolling. "Poor faithful old dog! The loss of this dear friend quite took the heart out of us and we did not feel like proceeding up the peak."

Even though it was nearly dark, the party took time to bury Fritz. Covering him with shale and moss, they erected a long slab of stone and inscribed "Fritz" with an ice axe on the improvised tombstone. Wheeler was not impervious to feelings of tenderness.

The purpose of the two-year Selkirk survey was to provide the ever-increasing number of climbers and explorers with accurate maps and information. But one season of exhilarating work so stimulated Wheeler's interest that the project became much more ambitious. With great dedication he undertook an intensive and immensely time-consuming program of research into the history of exploration in Canada's mountains and instead of gathering dust in official files, his report was published in 1905. *The Selkirk Range* is an excellent and most interesting account of all that was known about every aspect of the subject; it is lavishly illustrated and accompanied by a separate folio containing Wheeler's maps and copies of all previous maps of the area.

By the time it appeared in print, A. O. Wheeler was acquiring a reputation of distinction in the alpine world.

Chapter VIII

Wheeler's work in his Calgary office was interrupted in the spring of 1903 by a wire urging his immediate presence in Ottawa. W. F. King, Canadian Commissioner on the Alaska Boundary Commission, informed him that a report had been received "of alleged Russian monuments and ruins of an old stone house on the Dalton Trail to the Klondike..." As the Commission was to meet soon in London, the authenticity of the report had to be investigated on the spot. As he had been warned that the object of his visit was to be top secret, Wheeler and an assistant left Vancouver on a C.P.R. steamer, dressed "in knicker-bockers, golf stockings, Norfolk jackets, tweed caps...posing as tourists..."

It was "a wonderful trip". Embarking early in April, they were met at Skagway by the North West Mounted Police who escorted them to their destination. It was "a new experience travelling by dog-team", alternately riding on the sled and running on the ice. "There were many channels of open water to cross....The dogs...were crossed by chucking them in bodily, harness and all, to scramble out on the other side in a horrible tangle. The sleds were then carried across on our shoulders." Passing "Porcupine City", they arrived at "Pleasant Camp, just within Yukon Territory", the headquarters of the N.W.M.P. With Captain McDonnell and detachment "we enjoyed most happily the charming hospitality of Inspector and Mrs. McDonnell."

They moved on a few miles to "Rainy Hollow on the Dalton Trail..." where his instruments had been taken by dog team. There they found "a small shack ten feet square. Snow was up to the roof and the doorway had to be dug out...." It was "the only sign of life" in a desolate landscape and with six companions Wheeler spent thirteen days there. It was "a dirty hole, but better than a tent".

It was "but a short run to the supposed Russian stone house and so-called monuments." From brush shelters in the field it took him two nights to get astronomical observations; the temperature was near zero and he "found it beastly cold and uncomfortable." In biting wind, he "chained on snowshoes". Rising at 3:30 a.m., he worked in a blizzard: "Had taken no lunch. Felt fine after supper." Reminiscing years later, he wrote, "I was then in my prime and hardship in the great out-of-doors meant little to me."

He got the photographic data, developed his plates, and mapped and located the area. At each stop on the way back to Skagway he took time to bid farewell to friends he had made. He was back in Vancouver May 6th and rushed to Ottawa with his report. It was subsequently presented but had no significant bearing on the boundary settlement.

The same year he was appointed Topographer with the Department of the Interior and given the task of surveying the railway belt through the main range of the Rockies. The season's work began in the Lake Louise area and continued north along the Bow River to Bow Lake.

Hector and Oliver were working with the party again, "Oliver doing nice little rock climb by way of chimney." Also with the crew was a young graduate of the University of Toronto, Morrison Bridgland, who had been with Wheeler on the Selkirk survey—he too earned a reputation as a pioneer mountain surveyor.

Occupying stations above Bow Lake, Hector suffered severe chest pains and on Observation Peak he was very ill. Arthur was terrified he would die as "he was puffing for dear life." He dashed down to camp and returned with medicine and brandy. In a few days Hector was back at work.

Clara's health was also cause for concern. In photographs taken in Calgary in 1898 she looks frail and hollow-eyed; several earlier diary notes had reported: "Clara not well." He took her to the little chalet at Lake Louise and next day she "rode for the first time. Not used up." Undoubtedly he hoped that in those supremely beautiful and restful surroundings her health would improve. But in a few days she was sick in bed.

That summer Arthur and his men faced a heavy work load. Occupying fifty-seven camera stations, he took three hundred and five "views" from peaks at Bow, Moraine, and Sherbrooke Lakes, in Consolation and Paradise Valleys, and Lake Louise. By the end of the season, after many days working on cold ridges where he was often drenched to the skin for hours, his rheumatism was painful and he sought relief in the hot sulphur pools in Banff at Dr. Brett's Sanitarium. Dr. Brett, later Lieutenant Governor of Alberta, ran a very famous establishment, a large three-storey frame building surrounded with verandahs, and set in what is now the Administration Building grounds and park.

The lure of the mountains was so compelling by this time that he decided at the last minute to spend Christmas at Glacier House. Clara was summoned to join him. Tramping on the glaciers on snowshoes, he took "excellent winter views" of his beloved Selkirks; he helped Mrs. Young decorate the dining room, and on Christmas eve she "provided a jorum of mulled port" as they chatted comfortably round the cheery fire.

In 1904 the survey was carried from the Pipestone Valley to O'Hara, McArthur and Emerald Lakes. Clara's parents visited her in Calgary for the summer and the seventy-three-year old Professor went off to collect near the survey camps. He wandered on his own when camp was being moved from Kicking Horse summit to Field and was overtaken by a fierce thunderstorm as he tramped along the railway track. Lightning hummed ominously in the overhanging telegraph wires and he crawled under the ledge of the railway ties "to save my life". Next day he set off for Emerald Lake and after taking a wrong trail found his way to the Yoho Glacier, which Wheeler was measuring.

Arthur's father-in-law took a lively interest in his career. In 1902 he had suggested that he join the Royal Geographical Society; sponsored by Sir

Sandford Fleming, Wheeler was accepted as a fellow of the organization. Many of the late nineteenth-century explorers and climbers were also members and Wheeler had either met them in the course of his surveys or corresponded with them while gathering material for his Selkirk book.

His work was becoming well known and in 1904 he was invited to present a paper to the International Geographic Congress, meeting in Washington. His address on "Topographic Surveying by Means of Photography" was carried by Washington and New York papers. Very astutely he sent copies to leading Canadian papers, his Deputy Minister, and the Vice-President of the C.P.R.

He also arranged a display of his mountain photographs and maps at the Congress and in the Canadian Pavilion at the St. Louis World Fair. In a letter to his mother he described some highlights of this visit. "Canada has a number of fine exhibits at the Fair. The Canadian Headquarters was a tasty white stone...Lodge with a wide verandah, and lots of chairs for visitors from the Dominion....There were comfortable parlours for ladies and pictures of Canada and game heads decorating the walls. The Miner exhibit was excellent. In a rock grotto was...Klondyke gold with electric lights turned upon it. This glowed like a fiery furnace and could be seen the full length of the building...

"Another feature was the review of the Essex Fusiliers from Ontario....It filled you with a sense of security to see the long red lines of Tommies in the heart of the United States, and as the band struck up 'The Maple Leaf for Ever' and 'God Save the King' a feeling of home enveloped you and made you realize that you were not such a lost atom after all.

"The same evening I was dining with a friend—Prof. Parker of Columbia University—at the Chinese Restaurant, on the 'pike' corresponding to the 'Midway' at the Chicago World's Fair. All the shows are here and they are wonderful indeed on the outside....At night all the buildings are out-lined by myriads of coloured electric lamps. It looks like a gigantic fairy-land. A dense crowd surges up and down. Hundreds of Megaphones are shouting the different attractions... The eastern juggler with his 'Look! Look! See! See!' is everywhere. Ballet girls, Indians, Japanese, Elephants, Camels, Dwarfs, Negroes and all nationalities from all parts of the world are indiscriminately mixed....

"Well, as I was enjoying the mysteries of Chinese cooking...a dish of 'Chicken Chops Suez with Mushrooms' which is highly delectable...a sound of martial music rose above the din....Down the centre of the street, headed by three bands...[a] column four deep of the red-coated Essex Fusiliers, Arkansas Rangers and the blue-jacketed tars of the U.S. Navy....It was a wonderful sight and as the crowd opened to right and left to let them through, the people shouted and cheered: 'Here come the Canadians! Hurrah for the Canadians!'"

He couldn't begin to see all the exhibits which included Ireland, Tyrolean Alps, The Creation, The Hereafter, Japan, Ancient Rome, Baby Incubators, Cairo, Chinese Village, Cliff Dwellers, and Water Shutes. He did, however, see the Boer War one "which was excellent. Generals Cronje and Vil Joen were there and the men rode very well. The horses fell all round...and were trained to lie where they fell."

In May of 1905 he was a guest speaker at the Annual Meeting of the Appalachian Mountain Club in Boston. Clara accompanied him and they were royally entertained—the privileges of the Boston's Union Club were extended to him, and Professor Fay held an "At Home for Mr. and Mrs. A. O. Wheeler of Calgary, Canada."

Professor Fay had stopped over briefly at Glacier House in 1890; he had just enough time for a quick scramble up the slopes of Mount Sir Donald but the view of surrounding peaks was impressive—a vast array of virgin summits and glaciers to tempt climbers and explorers! His enthusiastic report to fellow members of the Appalachian Club aroused their interest. They came to participate in Canada's golden age of mountaineering.

Wheeler's interest in mountaineering as a recreational sport was aroused when he met Whymper in Banff and Mrs. Mary Schäffer at Glacier House. She was a cultivated Quaker woman from Philadelphia who had been coming to the Rockies for the summer since 1888, and she assisted his enthusiastic historical research for his book on the Selkirks. From the journals of the Appalachian and London Alpine Clubs he learned of the exploits of the witty Irish clergyman-climber, the Rev. Spotswood Green, and the engaging young Walter Wilcox and his Yale friends, who in the late 1890's began to seek out the hidden valleys of the main range of the Rockies. In 1901 he met the Rev. James Outram, who was to compete with the veteran British climber Professor Norman Collie in a race to the summit of the highest peaks in the range. He began a life-long friendship with Professor Fay.

Fay and Wheeler agreed that exciting discoveries awaited those who were eager to venture into unknown alpine terrain—exploration would flourish if an alpine club was organized to train climbers. Wheeler, as self-appointed public relations man for Canada's mountains, had already written a widely published article entitled, "Canadians as Mountaineers". It drew slight response because there were less than a dozen experienced mountaineers in Canada, and with a few exceptions they were surveyors. Under the circumstances he and Fay decided to form a North American Alpine Club with a Canadian branch. In 1905 Wheeler's article to this effect appeared in Canada's leading newspapers, including the *Manitoba Free Press*.

In very short order he received a copy of this article accompanied by another which took Wheeler "roundly to task, declared my actions were unpatriotic, chided my lack of imperialism and generally gave me a pen-lashing...."

The critic was a remarkable woman. Mrs. Elizabeth Parker was born and educated in Nova Scotia; after her marriage she moved to Winnipeg where she wrote a column and book reviews for the Winnipeg paper. In 1904 she spent eighteen months in Banff to regain her health and during that time acquired a deep and lasting love for the Rockies. She had reviewed Wheeler's Selkirk book, concluding her comments with an appeal for organized mountaineering in Canada.

On receipt of her criticism he wrote to her, saying he shared her patriotism, but as Canadian response had not been encouraging, would she use her talent and influence to arouse support? She replied that she certainly would, but only on behalf of an independent Canadian organization. She approached her famous editor, J. W. Dafoe, who responded with scant enthusiasm for the strenuous joys of mountain climbing, but the prospect of kindling national support for a Canadian endeavour appealed to him. He promised her that his influential editorial columns would support such a plan, but he was doubtful about any favourable reaction to her suggested appeal for Dominion

Government support. She made the attempt however, and Prime Minister Laurier "gave the proposed movement his benediction if nothing else"; the Minister of the Interior, Frank Oliver, was too busy to "give the matter his attention."

Even before he had heard of the extent of Mrs. Parker's efforts, Wheeler had decided to renew his campaign for Canadian support. By publicly questioning his patriotic fervour and imperialism Mrs. Parker had added impetus to this cause. Personal letters were sent to "prominent Canadians" which asked these questions: "Are you in favour of forming a Canadian section of an American Alpine Club and, if not, will you take an active part in a purely Canadian organization?" The questions were well worded. All public figures receiving the letter pledged firm support for a Canadian club. By March of 1906 the projected Alpine Club of Canada had seventy-seven charter members. "Nothing", Wheeler declared, "since the formation of the Lord Strathcona Horse has so appealed to the Canadian feeling for Empire."

It took a year of tireless effort to complete preparations for launching the Club, as Wheeler could not give his full attention to the work until the season's surveys were completed. His rheumatism plagued him again and in the autumn he returned to Banff for a session at the hot springs. Clara had spent the summer in the East with her family, and the Calgary cottage was rented, so he moved his office to Banff, establishing home and office at Grand View Villa, run by Nurse McColl; Clara joined him there in November.

He was delighted at the prospect of spending the winter in the tiny quiet mountain village. Clara may well have been less enchanted. On her first day the temperature was twelve below, the heat failed in Miss McColl's establishment and much of the day was spent fixing cracks in the walls in an attempt to keep out frigid drafts. But Christmas was a beautifully mild day and he drove Clara to church, helped Miss McColl with festive decorations, and enjoyed water polo before dinner.

As well as working on, or supervising the map work of Hector and Bridgland, he now started the extensive correspondence relating to the forthcoming inaugural meeting of the Alpine Club. Clara soon discovered that the combined office-home arrangement had distinct disadvantages. She was given "a lot of letters to type". With his unbounded enthusiasm and inexhaustible energy he failed to realize that others could not match his capacity for work. Clara undoubtedly made it clear that she was unable to do his secretarial work. His unmarried sister Kathleen was recruited to handle these duties, but home and office were soon moved back to Calgary.

He wrote to his mother about Banff. "I have been intending for a long time to write to you but for the past three weeks have been pretty helpless with rheumatism....I suppose by this time Clara will have written you that she is staying with the Rowleys while I am away....She also had quite a touch of grip and alone at home would have been horrible for her. It is not bad here at all. I have a nice bright room with two windows looking into the mountains. The grub is good, except that everything tastes of sulphur. We breathe it, eat it, drink it. Our thoughts are sulphurous. The air reeks of it, and the shrieks and groans of the suffering spirits who are parboiled daily in the pit, as we call the hot-water tub, gives the whole place the atmosphere of Hades.... Around this mouth of the Inferno are cold grey mountains, clad with pine... Please excuse a description that may be somewhat fantastic, but this is a fantastic spot... I suppose you know that Willie is again married... He seems to have struck a second treasure..."

When Willie had declined his brother's offer of employment, he did indeed exercise his talents in more congenial surroundings. In 1901 he married Edith Eleanor, sister of Senator Alfred Ernest Fripp. The Fripps occupied a comfortably high niche in Ottawa society and were not at all pleased about Edith's alliance to the charming, easy-going Willie. They paid the young couple an annuity to stay out of the country. This was quite agreeable to Willie who moved to California. Unhappily, his wife died in 1904 but Willie had no difficulty in finding "a second treasure" who freed him from tiresome concerns about earning a living.

In mid-February of 1906 Wheeler arranged to meet C.P.R. dignitaries at Field. He had convinced the Western Division Superintendent that an alpine club was a worthwhile enterprise and now he boldly approached the Second Vice-President of the Railway and requested Company assistance. When asked to state his needs, Wheeler promptly replied: "I want twenty passes to Winnipeg and return from any part of the Railway to bring delegates there to found an Alpine Club of Canada .... Mr. Whyte looked astounded, then incredulous, then scornful, as much as to say 'What confounded cheek!' Then he roared, 'Twenty passes to Winnipeg from any part of the Railway?' and turning to Mr. McPherson, he said....'What do you think of that, McPherson?' Mr. McPherson replied 'I think it would be a first-class idea Mr. Whyte.' 'All right' Mr. Whyte replied with a broad smile, 'Fix it up with him.'"

The founding meeting of the Club was held March 27th, 1906, in Winnipeg. The twenty-seven delegates elected Wheeler President and Mrs. Parker Secretary. She had used her influence to obtain an invitation for Wheeler to address the Canadian Club, and the members enthusiastically applauded his illustrated lecture on "The Wonderland of Canada." Mrs. Parker, the co-founder of the Club, remained an ardent spokesman of the Club for the rest of her life although she never climbed higher than the tree-line on Cascade Mountain in Banff.

Three of the charter members were clergymen. Rev. J. C. Herdman of Knox Presbyterian Church, Calgary, Very Reverend Dean Paget of Calgary, and Rev. C. W. Gordon (one of Canada's most widely read novelists of the day who wrote under the pseudonym of Ralph Connor) had all climbed in Switzerland and Canada. Herdman became Vice-President as did Dr. A. P. Coleman of Toronto, Professor of Geology. Dr. Coleman and his brother (also a charter member) had explored extensively in the Rockies, blazing the trail from the Sunwapta River to Jasper along what is now the famous Banff-Jasper highway. Sir Sandford Fleming was elected Honourary President; plans were formulated for the first Alpine Club camp, and the aims of the organization were defined.

The primary objective of the Club was not to provide training and recreation for mountaineers. Very high on the list of priorities was the promotion of the historical and scientific study of the mountains, efforts to attract artists who would depict alpine scenery, and, above all, a campaign to make Canadians aware of the extent and grandeur of their mountain heritage.

Wheeler's zeal for spreading "the gospel of the mountains" had another dimension, springing from his education at Dulwich. Not only would mountaineering "harden the muscles and make elastic the sinews," it would produce

*A group photograph taken at the official
founding of the Alpine Club of Canada. A. O.
Wheeler is third from the left in the front row,
standing beside Mrs. Elizabeth Parker.*

men with high ideals, capable of "moral greatness". Climbing was "the sport of intellectuals", as the English club's membership testified—their great pioneers were "men of refinement", probably because "a passion for the high mountains requires some measure of poetic imagination, a love of beauty for its own sake and the appreciation of achievement totally unrelated to any tangible rewards."

Without this fervour an organization as novel and impractical as a Canadian Alpine Club would never have got off the ground. It flourished because of Wheeler's initiative, energy, and commitment. In the early 1900s world travellers on the C.P.R. knew more about the Rockies than most Canadians, who considered them to be as remote as Afghanistan.

By the time the first camp was held in the summer of 1906, Wheeler had persuaded "well-known leaders in various communities of this great Dominion to lend their influence and financial support." Grants were received from the federal and provincial governments; the Department of the Interior paid the salaries of Wheeler and his survey assistants, Bridgland and Hector, for the time required to set up and direct camp. The C.P.R. loaned the services of their Swiss guides and cooks from their chalets and hotels, and extended half-fair privileges to Club members travelling to camp. The N.W.M.P.

at Banff and Calgary loaned tents and camp equipment, and local packtrain outfitters provided free service. This assistance allowed the Club to charge very nominal fees, making it possible for many Canadians of modest means to vacation in their mountains.

Wheeler saw to it that press representatives from Canada's largest centres were Club guests—they came, saw, photographed, and their lavishly illustrated articles appeared in newspapers and periodicals. Those communities not sending representatives were showered with his own press releases. For years Alpine Club activities were newsworthy, not only in Canada but in the United States.

It took a great deal of organizational ability and sheer hard work to set up and run a camp situated in mountain wilderness miles from the railway and accommodating hundreds of people. Thirty or forty tents, enormous amounts of food (each day's meals consumed fifteen sides of bacon, four hams, eighty loaves of bread, innumerable tins of produce and jams), and tools and utensils had to be hauled in by packtrain. In later years, when camps were deep in the hinterland, ground and paths had to be cleared, dining-tent tables and benches constructed, poles cut, and tents set up with balsalm-bough beds expertly made for each one. Wheeler conducted each day's activities with military efficiency and discipline which was mitigated by his amiable manner and the easy camaraderie induced by the isolation and grandeur of the surroundings.

For those who attended, the first camp remained an indelible memory. They left the railway at Field on July 8th. A handful of tenderfeet rode in the democrat which met the train to transport luggage, but most set out on foot in a long line to cross the flats of the Kicking Horse River. Very few had seen the mountains before and the great towering precipices, castellated crags and ice-capped summits were awesome. It was sunrise, and the dew of night had washed sky and earth—all the alpine splendour looked clean, fresh, new. The forest trail to Emerald Lake was cool, quiet, scented with the pines which formed a cathedral aisle; at its head a noble peak lifted its glistening crown of snow into an intensely blue sky. They passed Emerald Lake, where the unruffled turquoise-green water clearly reflected forest-skirted peaks, and made their way to Yoho Pass.

Soon A. O. Wheeler overtook them, "loping along on his pony, as easy a rider as ever sat a saddle." With satisfaction he greeted this large contingent of "pilgrims with 'Exelsior' written on face and eye", and hurried ahead to be on hand when they reached their destination. He may have had momentary apprehensions about shepherding to mountain tops lady-hopefuls dressed in floor-length gowns and dainty hats. A "wag of a trail guide drawled, 'Say Boss! Get yer eye on them outfits.... They're fierce! And they were...." Men with Derby hats and summer straws, some carrying umbrellas! But he "soon licked them into shape". As he himself would not be climbing, he was trimly turned out in Norfolk jacket, knickerbockers, navy and white polka dot tie, and an informal fedora, carefully creased to resemble a jaunty tyrolean hat.

What the weary but expectant travellers found awaiting them was a neat tent village situated just beyond the high saddle of the Yoho Pass, and surrounded by lush forest. The sunny upper alplands were carpeted with wildflowers—all the pristine beauty seemed undisturbed by the footsteps of man.

Clara Wheeler, Julia Henshaw and A. O.
Wheeler at Alpine Club camp.

Newcomers were directed to the President's administrative tent, where he welcomed them officially and assigned sleeping quarters. In the tea tent nearby they were greeted by Clara. Frail but diligent, she presided as hostess, and at any time of day or evening she had the indispensable tea ready for tired climbers and listened with keen interest to their experiences of the day. In the camp photograph she is seated amid rugged mountaineers, serenely beautiful in a large, softly-draped hat, long skirt, shirtwaist blouse and tie.

Occupying the central spot in the clearing, great logs were ready for the evening campfire; there was a large open-fronted dining tent, one for photographic displays, and on each side separate paths led to ladies' and gentlemen's sleeping quarters nestled in the fringe of forest. Prominent signs of each day's climbing or hiking were displayed on tree bulletin boards and those intending to climb were roused at 4 a.m. by the President's cheery call at their tent. After a breakfast of strong coffee and bacon they lined up before him for roll call, where terse instructions were issued and genial good wishes extended.

Climbers were not allowed to go without a guide. To the novices, 10,900 foot Mount Vice-President must have seemed awesomely inaccessible. But under the guidance of Swiss guides, surveyors Bridgland and Hector, and assisted by Oliver, many made their graduating climb on its forbidding cliffs.

Even the ladies who wore absurdly voluminous bloomers in camp, set a commendable record—fifteen did the climb and others in long skirts and frilly hats were soon glissading merrily down snowy slopes.

The blazing campfire invited good fellowship. Each evening experiences were exchanged and tales of witty raconteurs enjoyed; someone would throw a giant log on the embers and showers of sparks would shoot into the starry sky; lingering until eyelids drooped, the ladies would begin to leave as gentlemen gallantly sang "Good Night Ladies". Sunday services were conducted there, where the scenery encouraged a feeling of reverence and worship.

When, at week's end the refreshed contingent left with many a backward glance at the land of enchantment they were leaving, Wheeler, Hector, and Oliver dismantled camp and hurried back to work, where they found the men happily playing cards. With a scorching tongue-lashing they were hustled back to neglected tasks.

Earlier in the season the survey was carried into Ptarmigan Valley, northeast of Lake Louise, and after the Club camp, work began on the peaks overlooking the Amiskwi, Ottertail, Ice River, Kootenay, and Beaverfoot valleys.

Wheeler was aware from his study of mountain history that he was mapping in terrain where early explorers had travelled, and before the summer was over he understood only too well the adversities they had encountered. Again and again his diary notes refer to arduous forays into almost impenetrable forests where they were caught in "a horrid tangle" of underbrush. "Pretty hard day all round." One day they covered only a mile even though all hands were strenuously cutting trail; it was often "tough travelling" even for horses in the Beaverfoot Valley or clambering over steep Baker Pass. To reach peaks with instruments, they cut a total of twenty-four miles of trail through thick timber, but ninety-eight camera stations were occupied and over five hundred plates exposed.

On his return to Calgary he met Sir Sandford Fleming, who invited him to make an examination of the cement works at Exshaw. He and Clara travelled in Fleming's private railway car and the two men enjoyed a game of chess on the homeward journey. When they parted Wheeler had his host's commitment to write a very interesting article for the first edition of the *Canadian Alpine Journal*.

Chapter IX

1907 was a fruitful year and even by A. O. Wheeler's exacting standards, one of strenuous activity. He and Clara had spent Christmas with their families, with Arthur frantically writing his address for the prestigious Canadian Club lecture circuit early in the new year. His youngest sister, Josephine, had married the Rev. George Jacob Bousfield, and his mother lived with them; Oliver joined his parents and there were family reunions with both Wheelers and Macouns.

Arriving back in his Calgary office in the new post office building, he started work immediately on reports and mapping. The map work was urgent; the influx of tourists was rising at a gratifying rate and the C.P.R. was ordering hundreds of copies for distribution in their hotels and chalets. He spent nearly every evening and Sunday afternoons dealing with an enormous amount of correspondence. For over a year he had been personally canvassing for contributions (including a request to the Governor General) to erect "a handsome marble monument" at Lake Louise station to honour explorer-geologist Sir James Hector. He wrote hundreds of letters to potential Alpine Club members and as editor, solicited articles from carefully chosen authorities for the *Canadian Alpine Journal*.

Before surveys began Wheeler received publicity from an unexpected quarter. On May 30th, when mountain snows were still deep, he took C. W. Rowley, Manager of the Calgary branch of the Bank of Commerce, a C.P.R. executive, and a Swiss guide, Peter Kaufmann, to Paradise Valley to select the Alpine Club campsite. Wheeler and Kaufmann escorted Rowley to the summit of Mount Aberdeen.

This feat made a splendid anecdote which was widely circulated at the Alberta Hotel's bar. Shortly it appeared in Calgary's notorious *Eye Opener*. As usual, editor-publisher Bob Edwards gave the tale his individual touch.

The article began with details of Mr. Rowley's accomplishment and went on to say that inasmuch as the only exercise the bank manager had taken for three years was to walk the short distance from his home to the bank, where he indulged in the strenuous "juggling of tables of interest and balancing columns of figures", it was most commendable that he should

Club members making an ascent at the Paradise Valley camp.

undertake the scramble in order to leave his bank's calling card on the summit. This was an admirable example of English pluck and endurance and gave his bank the distinction of having its advertisement on the highest point in Canada. Just *why* he chose this mode of advertising, however, "The Lord only knows.... Comparatively few pedestrians pass that way so only God will see it and this is rather pointless for He doesn't bank at The Commerce."

Few Calgarians of Wheeler's and Rowley's class would admit to being readers of Edwards' paper. But many of them enjoyed it, even if the pretensions of "society" were a most frequent target of the editor's ridicule. Wheeler had met Edwards at Dr. Brett's sanitarium when the editor was recuperating from another bout with the bottle (other notable Calgarians often "took the cure" there) and "found him a very fine man to talk to". Irreverant Edwards certainly was, but Wheeler, like many others, found him a gentle, humane and cultivated man. His newspaper gave Wheeler staunch support in his subsequent battle with the Minister of the Interior.

Due to late spring snowfalls the campsite selected had to be changed at the last minute. The C.P.R.'s Calgary Passenger Agent sent workmen to bridge a swollen stream, cut new paths, and assist Wheeler, Bridgland, Hector and Oliver to carve a new campground out of virgin forest in Paradise Valley. When 150 members arrived, white tents mushroomed on the larch-studded meadow at the foot of Horseshoe Glacier beneath the mighty ramparts of Mount Hungabee. For a glorious week they climbed and hiked to nearby Lake O'Hara and Moraine Lake. At the Annual Meeting round the campfire they heard the President report on his activities. Money raised during his lecture tour had been added to the exchequer, and as a great honour to the Club, he had been invited to attend the Jubilee celebrations of the Alpine Club in London.

With initiative and assiduous effort, Wheeler was beginning to fulfill ambition to make the Club "one of the world's premier alpine organizations." He recruited the very large membership by writing letters to alpinists in Australia, South Africa, France, England, Ireland, and the United States. As British and American climbers had been actively interested in Canada's mountains for years, he sent copies of his *Selkirk Range* to them, as well as news of Club activities in their journals. The influential Whymper held Wheeler in high regard—in 1908 he proposed him as Honourary Member of the English Club, an exceedingly rare tribute.

Oliver had assisted at camp and again joined his father on the survey. He had come directly from graduation exercises at Trinity College School. Newspapers reported that he had been the "hero of the afternoon"; he was called back to the platform again and again to receive awards and prizes, including the Chancellor's prize and Governor General's silver medal for general proficiency; his companions, who had elected him as the young man most deserving of recognition for his consistent "integrity, courtesy and industry" applauded with vigour.

Bridgland's party was instructed to work south from Golden along the Columbia River valley, occupying stations in the Dogtooth Mountains and Beaverfoot Range, while Wheeler, Oliver, Hector, and their assistants pushed into the Spillimacheen mountains. Both parties were hindered by foul weather. Bridgland worked only thirty miles in the valley—it had been hoped he could complete the survey to the junction of the Kootenay River. Instead, his party was called back to complete work north from the Kicking Horse valley and up the Blaeberry River.

Wheeler's men forced trails to stations through abominably heavy timber and undergrowth; he often preceded the men, cutting trail for them. Many diary entries refer to a 5 a.m. start up the slopes: "Very hard day. Very tired." Occasionally he and Oliver were in high camps in snow and hailstorms and at one point "there was little grub. No meat or bread in camp." On days when photographical conditions were good they climbed through humid forests where swarming mosquitoes and black flies attacked viciously. In October snows Wheeler and Bridgland made a traverse up the Blaeberry and along the railway from Donald to Beavermouth.

The season of bad weather was exceptionally frustrating that year because it prevented Wheeler's examination of the Spillimacheen mountains. "Between the North and South branches of the Spillimacheen River and southward" he had glimpsed "a magnificent tract of truly Alpine country with wide icefields...sharp peaks, snow-clad domes and precipices in the wildest confusion.... This tract is practically unknown...." The lure of the unknown!

When the season ended "forty peaks had been climbed, seventy-seven camera stations occupied and thereon...471 plates exposed" and data collected "to enable the mapping of more than a thousand square miles of mountain country." After seven seasons in the Rockies and Selkirks Wheeler had enough material "to furnish topographical maps of the mountain area lying along both sides of the Canadian Pacific Railway between the Gap at the eastern escarpment and Revelstoke at the second crossing of the Columbia River."

On returning to the Calgary office, he found copies of the first issue of the *Canadian Alpine Journal* ready to mail and copies were rushed off to be in the hands of the British alpinists before he arrived for the Jubilee.

For years the *Canadian Alpine Journal* ("one of the largest and most profusely illustrated books ever published in the West") has contained not only reports of the annual camp but scientific accounts dealing with alpine botany, zoology, geology, and reports on the movement of glaciers; it has carried reviews of alpine literature, articles about exploration, mountaineering and Canadian alpine history.

He and Clara had their usual November picnic for his survey crew; then he dashed to Banff for therapy in the pools and late in November left for the East.

He visited his mother. Mrs. Wheeler must have been deeply moved by the thought that the Wheeler heir was returning to visit the land of his birth. He had already received inquiries about the sale of the estates, but out of consideration for her he may not have mentioned this. To remind him of his heritage she told him that she was leaving him "the Wheeler Communion Cup" in her will, a companion piece to the famous Elizabethan Flagon Bishop Wheeler had received. As a special favour he photographed it for her and she presented framed copies to her children as Christmas gifts.

Sailing from New York, he arrived just in time for the three-day celebrations and meetings. He was delighted to meet the men whose books he had read: Rev. W. S. Green, the first British climber to explore and map in the Selkirks near Glacier House; the amiable Professor Collie, and the wryly-humourous Stutfield, authors of *Climbs and Explorations in the Canadian Rockies*. Collie had led four expeditions into the area north of Lake Louise and, with Stutfield and their good friend, Herman Woolley, had discovered the vast Columbia Icefields. Undoubtedly Wheeler had animated discussions with them about the immense extent of mountain terrain still to be explored. The Alps were becoming almost hackneyed and explorers were venturing to the distant Caucasus and Himalayas in search of adventure. But because the Rockies were easily accessible by rail, expeditions were within the modest means of professors and clergymen who were such active members of the Club.

When he learned that the British Association for the Advancement of Science would be holding its meeting in Canada in 1909 (many alpinists were members of the Association), he immediately invited them to be guests of the Canadian Alpine Club at camp.

He spent Christmas in London with his cousin, Dr. Hugh Helsham, who had been at Dulwich with him, and on the 28th dashed off for his only visit to the Alps. Frank Bergne, son of Sir Henry Bergne (a member of the English Club who had been to Canada) had arranged a guided climb of the Ulrichshorn. The party of nine, including three guides, set out on New Years Day. Tramping over icefields, they climbed uneventfully until dusk when they came to a difficult precipice. They roped up but Mr. Bergne confidently refused the rope. Within minutes he plunged to his death. Dazed and horrified, his companions abandoned the climb.

Wheeler was 'miserable' and shaken by the tragedy. They spent the night in a hut nearby, hoping to participate in the rescue next day. But it turned hot and danger of avalanches ruled out any attempt to retrieve the body. Wheeler had to leave. On his return he called immediately to offer condolences to the bereaved parents.

As soon as he arrived in Ottawa he visited his mother to tell her about his experiences in England and Ireland. Oliver, who was attending Royal Military College at Kingston, joined them.

Her grandchildren retained a vivid memory of Mrs. Wheeler. A stately figure in sombre Victorian dress with a touch of lace on the collar, a tiny white cap resting on snowy hair, pince-nez dangling on a black ribbon—an old woman, comfortably immobile, sitting serenely for hours by a window or in the garden. As Arthur spoke of her homeland what memories stirred, ebbed, and flowed into focus? A proud and vivacious young lady of the manor...carefree days at Desart Court...balls at Kilkenny Castle...regret? Hopes that the Wheeler heir might yet take his place on ancestral estates? Or would this handsome and promising eighteen-year-old grandson win the honours Wheelers had enjoyed for centuries?

Five weeks later in his Calgary office, Arthur received an urgent telegram: "Must come at once." He was too late. At the Kenora station Hector's wire awaited him. His mother had died the previous day.

She was buried in All Saints Cemetery on the outskirts of Collingwood. As the black-plumed hearse made its way along the bleak wintery roadway, a teamster's sleigh came toward them. Courtesy demanded that he make way for the cortege. He insolently refused and the driver leapt out and forced the obstructing horses into the ditch. The procession went on its way with the outraged workman shouting blasphemous imprecations in its wake.

Under the terms of her will, Mrs. Wheeler's married daughters, Bessie and Josephine, each inherited a quarter of the income and property left to her by her father, and Kathleen received the other half. Captain Wheeler's estates passed to Arthur—they had been held by the Marquess of Ormonde only until Captain Wheeler and his wife died.

Arthur sold the estates. He would put down new roots in western Canada. Formalities of the sale were not complete until early in 1910 and by then the bustling city of Calgary was at the height of a frantic land boom. As usual, fortunes were made and lost. His estates brought him nearly eleven thousand dollars—a considerable sum at the time—and he invested part of it in twenty-seven acres on the western outskirts above the Bow River. So great was his confidence in the immediate potential of Calgary, that he urged his sisters to participate in the venture. Josephine had complete faith in his judgment and allowed him to risk her inheritance. Unhappily the land had to be sold when depression followed the boom. The loss was a serious blow to Josephine who had intended to use the money to educate her sons. She was too loyal to the brother she looked upon as a father to make an issue of the fact that Arthur had implied that he would provide financial assistance for this purpose should it be necessary. But the family felt that he had not fulfilled an obligation. In 1910, however, the balance of his inheritance provided a comfortable cushion of security when he made a crucial professional decision.

When he and Hector returned from their mother's funeral, survey instructions for the 1908 season were in his Calgary office. On April 20th three survey parties were placed in the field. Undoubtedly Wheeler would have preferred to continue the work of the previous season into the unexplored and tantalizing "Dogtooth Mountains". Instead, he was directed to classify the land within the Railway Belt of British Columbia, to ascertain the feasibility of settlement, and the potential for lumbering, mining, fishing, and orchard development.

The Alpine Club camp of 1908 was pitched on the summit meadow of Rogers Pass. Because of its historical significance for "the great National Enterprise' (the construction of the railway), Wheeler extended a special invitation to the very eminent Sir William Cornelius Van Horne. A handwritten refusal pleaded the pressure of work but the note was embellished with a delightfully witty caricature which graphically explained why a mountaineering camp would not be enhanced by his presence.

The day camp opened, eighteen-year-old Oliver (assisted by P. D. McTavish and the Rev. A. M. Gordon, both splendid experienced climbers, and the noted English alpinist, G. E. Howard) was leading a party of three on Mount Avalanche. The ascent was not difficult but even before any real climbing began, Oliver asked the two women of the party to wait above while he descended an easy snow slope. The precaution was one any responsible climber assumes. He had only started down when one girl shouted. "Look out, I'm coming!" Full of confidence and exhilaration, she began to run, lost her footing and, with increasing velocity, shot past him. Reacting instantly, he reached out to grab her. She was inches beyond his reach. In a split second she fell over a precipice. She was dead when her horrified companions reached her.

A thorough examination of the scene of the tragedy and an inquest concluded that "the calamity was not through any fault or negligence of any person in the party. Very especially we express the greatest confidence in the guide, Mr. Oliver Wheeler, one of our experienced guides who was leading the party most carefully."

Very wisely, as soon as the rescue team arrived, the party asked Oliver to lead them to the summit to demonstrate their trust in him.

When camp broke up, Bridgland returned to his survey in the Columbia Valley, Oliver accompanied his father on the Shuswap Lake work, and Hector was in charge of the men surveying north and south of Revelstoke. Though the lake country lacked the rugged magnificence of the Rockies and Selkirks it had its own particular beauty and fascination. There were no challenging climbs to beckoning summits but there was ample opportunity to enjoy mastery of oar and sail. The broad expanse of the water was often as calm as a sheet of glass, mirroring the timbered hills, but occasionally Wheeler had a "stiff row" at night when the lakes were lashed by storms.

He had befriended officials of one of the many timber companies in the area who gave him free use of their gasoline launch to move camps. One Sunday the motor would not start, because, as Wheeler thought, the battery was wet. A passing train crew took his order for a replacement to Revelstoke, but when it didn't arrive, he hopped on the train and got one himself, confident that he could get the launch going. After fruitless hours he succeeded in "setting the blame thing on fire. Gave it up. Hopeless." The fire was easily doused. Horses, sails and oars he could master but the vagaries of machinery remained an irritating enigma.

Hector's work was very arduous and the blazing heat exhausting. It was the first time he had complete responsibility for leading a party. In November, long treks and camps in snow-filled forests were the order of the day. At the end of the season all three parties met at Revelstoke where the outfit was loaded on a waiting freight. Amid the bustle Hector fainted on the station platform. Arthur carried him into the waiting room and placed him on a bench. When he revived, Arthur dashed to catch the train.

In a few days he received news that Hector was in the Revelstoke hospital. Arthur requested regular bulletins of his progress. After four months he had regained strength to travel East where he convalesced with Josephine and her husband at the Rectory near Ottawa. Hector had great strength of will which enabled him to endure the exacting demands and strenuous physical work his brother demanded. Physically frail, he could not withstand the complications which developed from over-exertion in the field. He never returned to his beloved mountains although to the last he remained quietly optimistic. When Arthur brought a carefully packed box of prairie anemones to his sickbed, he remarked, "They'll be beginning to bloom when we get to the O'Hara camp; but I shall not be climbing this year."

He was thirty-five years old when he died on July 6th, a few days before camp opened. The girl he would have married if he had enjoyed better health died soon after. Josephine Bousfield, her good friend, maintained that Edith Bray died of a broken heart.

When he had visited Hector it seemed likely that Wheeler himself wouldn't be at camp that year. In fact, newspaper reports were saying that there wouldn't be any camp.

Chapter X

A fine contingent of English climbers and members of the British Association for the Advancement of Science had accepted Wheeler's invitation to visit the Rockies for the 1909 Alpine Club camp. He planned to make it a memorable occasion. The clubhouse at Banff would be ready, and the O'Hara campsite was one of unsurpassable beauty. As an impressive climax, the guests were to be taken on a week's excursion through some of the most beautiful alpine scenery on the continent.

In his survey instructions for the year, Frank Oliver, Minister of the Interior, had instructed the Surveyor General that Wheeler was not to be allowed time off to attend Alpine Club camp with his assistants. To Wheeler this was incredible and outrageous. In short order newspapers were showered with press releases expressing righteous indignation. "We cannot overestimate the importance of the attendance of the British guests....[The presence of] some of the world's most eminent scientists and explorers will provide an opportunity to create a favourable impression of our Dominion....What an ugly advertisement for Canada if word goes forth that 'We cannot receive you as our guests; there will be no camp this year because the Government refuses the minimum of assistance required.'" In this impetuous retort, Wheeler, typically, ignored the fact that it was not the Government which had issued the invitation.

As this promised to be a spirited encounter, editors gave the controversy good coverage and some editorial support. The attack was to be carried to "the Dominion House if necessary...", Wheeler thundered. A flurry of correspondence went out to all Club members and influential acquaintances, urging them to protest to their Members of Parliament. One zealous partisan went so far as to question Mr. Oliver's competence. Clearly, anyone who failed to appreciate the accomplishments of the Alpine Club in bringing Canada such extensive promotion was unfit for the post of Minister of the Interior. Wheeler won the first round. He and his men were given permission to supervise the all-important camp.

Wheeler's clash with Oliver was not motivated primarily by a wish for self-aggrandizement. His background stressed the obligation of a host and he was always eager to share as widely as possible the unique recreational pleasures to be found in the mountains.

In May he began a season of frenzied activity. His own and two other parties took up the survey in the areas where they had worked the year before. He was so anxious to have his field work well in hand as soon as possible that he forged ahead at a terrific pace. In a few days he was "very tired and sore." For five weeks he scurried back and forth from Banff to the field. On Sundays he would be in to see that the clubhouse building was proceeding satisfactorily and he pitched in with the axe to clear the grounds. He and Oliver prepared the O'Hara campsite, dashed to Calgary to order supplies, and deployed these at various caches on the route of the high-trail excursion. Back in the field, a day beginning at 4 a.m. ended at dusk and he "slept badly." But when the first guests began arriving in Banff, he felt that he had "things in good order."

The clubhouse was ready and he proudly ran up the Union Jack. He had selected the site with care. High above the village on the slopes of Sulphur Mountain, the bright red roof amid the sombre pines made the headquarters of the Alpine Club of Canada a conspicuous landmark. Nearly two hundred guests came to the opening ceremony. From the encircling verandah or the windows of the second floor library, they looked out on a glorious panorama of peaks silhouetted against a sky washed with gold by the setting sun. And in the spacious assembly room, where great logs blazed in the massive stone fireplace, they sang round the piano and danced the night away.

Among the stars of the alpine world who came were the eminent statesman, Leopold S. Amery, Geoffrey Hastings, Godfrey Solly, and A. L. Mumm, the champagne magnate who journeyed to the world's highest peaks accompanied by his personal Swiss guide, Moritz Inderbinen. They were the first to arrive and were amazed to hear that the clubhouse had been an unbroken mountain slope a few months before. Along the paths under the pines, tent houses provided comfortable sleeping quarters, and the distinguished guests soon discovered that Clara combined "the onerous offices of quartermaster general and guardian angel of the Club."

In June, the endearing young Austrian guide, Conrad Kain, came directly from Europe to Banff and worked for Wheeler, first at the clubhouse, then at Camp and on the survey. When Wheeler arrived on one of his hurried supervisory visits to Banff, he immediately set to work like a labourer. Conrad, accustomed to rigid class distinction between employer and employee, protested that he would complete the work. Wheeler retorted: "I do my own share of work, Conrad. I am not a European." (This represents a sharp contrast with the attitude of his mother who forbade her daughters to say more than "Goodday" to people "in trade".) Any interested club member who strolled up to see how work was proceeding was expected to do the same—he was allotted a task in short order if the President was on hand!

Oliver's help was indispensable that hectic summer. He, Conrad, and a splendid English climber, Val Fynn, and young club volunteers left with a pack-train of thirty-five horses to put the O'Hara camp in order. Conrad noted that every evening they "were almost dead from fatigue", but in six days the alpine meadow blossomed with sixty bell tents where two hundred people were housed for a week.

The C.P.R. ran a special train to Hector station at Wapta Lake, where the alpinists set out on a four-hour walk up the valley "whose beauty would be difficult to rival anywhere in the world," as one participant quickly noted. And at the end of the forest trail, they saw the exquisite lake in its setting of snow-capped peaks— "a panorama that would remain imprinted on the memory for a lifetime."

Incomparable alpine splendour and the zeal of their host certainly impressed the twenty special guests from overseas, and they found the novel aspects of Canadian alpinism interesting and worthy of appreciation. The climbing was definitely enhanced by the presence of so many ladies—the English Club did not admit ladies. Furthermore the ladies wore "knickerbockers! Not short skirts with knickerbockers demurely projecting beneath, or baggy divided garments pretending to look like a skirt, but *good, honest ordinary* knickerbockers." The delighted observer "ventured to say that this was very satisfying to the aesthetic sense for anyone who has once got accustomed to the natural grace of a healthy, athletic girl in garments which give every movement of the limbs free play...." A remarkably unrestrained observation from an Edwardian gentleman!

Mumm's guide, Moritz Inderbinen, was much less enthusastic about lady mountaineers. He took one to the summit of Mount Huber and had ample time to wonder just how he had been persuaded to "volunteer" his service for this particular climb. Accustomed to the companionship of his master, whose agility and skill were so challenging, using the rope only for security—here he was, Moritz Inderbinen, "the gentleman's guide", in the role of a draught horse with the rope taut as he pulled his plump, aspiring climber across the snow slope! Conrad and his party passed him, and Inderbinen, looking exhausted, implored him: "Meet me with a lantern, for I need another two hours to the peak and have to pull already!"

The engaging and handsome Conrad enjoyed his feminine companions. While they waited out a storm on a bleak cliff he beguiled them with tales, and to add warmth and restore confidence, he bestowed "a little kiss" on demure cheeks. This manifestation of European romance and charm, added to his appealing accent, brought bevies of ladies to parties he led.

Four intrepid women participated in the spectacular excursion Wheeler arranged as a fitting climax for the British visitors. At its conclusion he admitted: "It was something of a feat"—a six-day hike around the rim of the Yoho Valley.

The ten guests were accompanied by twenty-three stalwart Alpine Club volunteers who conducted them from Hector station up the Sherbrooke Valley. Oliver and Bridgland were dispatched early to prepare the night's camp. Wheeler was at the Hector station to speed tardy strollers on their way, assuring them that if they hurried they would catch up to the pack-train which would relieve them of their packs. But the hikers soon discovered that the trail through the woods "was as conspicuous by its absence as the underbrush was by its presence." When they caught up to the horses they found "Equerry Jimmy Simpson riding last". One observer found him "a most entertaining and instructive companion. His control over the animals struck me as wonderful. When one of them went wrong he rated it, either by its individual name or by names (also used in England) of a more general and forcible application, and the offenders invariably returned promptly...."

The view of lady climbers in knickerbockers which an English visitor found so aesthetically appealing.

Wheeler had over-estimated the distance the walkers could make on the first day and they had to halt near timberline beyond Sherbrooke Lake. A violent thunderstorm crashed round them just as the pack-train was being unloaded and the horses stampeded. Nonetheless, in an incredibly short time they were brought under control, tents were pitched, fires blazed, and the evening meal was ready. Wheeler's diary notes: "Slept under a tree myself."

Next morning the travellers "realized the full extent of the generosity of our Canadian hosts." For two days, on the eastern part of the journey, they would make their way across terrain which was impassable for horses. The pack-train had been sent back and all personal kits and every necessity for camp was packed on the backs of Club volunteers. Each carried sixty or seventy pound loads.

In sweltering heat they ascended to Niles Pass; they had lunch in a summit blizzard with hail cutting their faces; in single file they negotiated the Daly Glacier and camped above timberline at the most northerly icefall of the glacier. Wheeler considered the "camp not bad, but turned a little cold at night"! As usual he was up early, supervising breakfast and sending his boys off with packs. At 7:30 he had his guests on the trail as well. Some dauntless climbers ascended the summit of Mount Balfour while the rest crossed the western slope and descended to the Yoho Glacier where they reached "a delightful camp in the forest", a half mile beyond the icefall.

Wheeler acknowledged that during those two days "some discomfort was experienced by our visitors but all were excellent sports and met all difficulties with the most cheery good humour...." This comment says a great deal about host and guests. Wheeler had expected everyone to endure the strenuous pace he set for himself. Conrad Kain recalled that Wheeler was livid with rage when the experienced guide, Jim Simpson, hadn't minced words when he soundly condemned the whole excursion. Kain agreed, and undoubtedly so did many who shouldered the loads. However, the pack-train met them and they tramped happily to camp on succeeding nights in Waterfall Valley, Summit and Emerald lakes.

The guests, too, were concerned about the heavy packs their Canadian companions were carrying; some insisted on doing their share. One of these was a merry English septuagenarian. Encumbered with his load, he waded a mountain torrent and slipped on a boulder. "With great agility he scrambled out of the water and having the heart of a boy for all his seventy years, he treated the episode as the best joke in the world. Nor did he fail to amuse the rest of the party when he issued from his tent later on, his lower man encased in a sleeping bag, as if the programme of the evening was likely to include a sack race." However, when the festivities round the magic circle of the campfire were over and the gay traveller joined his companions in their tent (where they had just fitted themselves "into our allotted spaces like sardines in a box"), the President and Vice-President called on him: "the President carrying his private flask of 'medicine' (we were a strictly temperance camp) and the Vice-President with a rug; the one to offer the 'Old Man' a warming cordial and the other to tuck him up in an extra blanket in case his cold bath had given him a chill."

Wheeler's great plans had been "most happily carried out, thanks to the good temper, willingness for hard work and readiness to be pleased with everything, by everyone concerned." This was his tribute to those who certainly deserved it. The excursion ended with a carriage ride from Emerald Lake to Field where they would entrain for the Association meetings in Winnipeg. On their last evening there was a great farewell banquet at Mount Stephen House where "'the Prince of Hosts' was roundly toasted...."

Many years later, recalling the expedition, Wheeler noted with amusement: "At its conclusion our guests said they had never done anything like it before and, *sotto voce,* hoped they would never do anything like it again."

When his guests departed he was exhausted. He returned to dismantle the O'Hara camp, made a quick trip to see how the survey was going, and prepared for his own illustrated address to the British Association meetings in Winnipeg. The festivities there included a reception at Government House and a garden party at Silver Heights, home of Donald Smith, Lord Strathcona.

Oliver, on his way back to Kingston, stopped over to hear his father's lecture. How proud Wheeler had been when Oliver and Val Fynn had succeeded in their guideless climb of Mount Hungabee — "the grim chieftain of Paradise Valley" — and what a triumph to see him hoisted on the shoulders of his friends to receive the congratulations of everyone at the O'Hara campfire.

From Winnipeg he hurried back to Banff. The C.P.R. was running a special train to the Pacific for the British Association members, with sightseeing stops in the mountains. When they arrived he was on hand to conduct their tours at Banff, Lake Louise, and Glacier House.

Letters of appreciation began to arrive from departed guests. Harold Dixon remarked that Wheeler's invitation had stipulated that "we will show you a good time...and we have had a *very* good time." A delightfully amusing letter from Mumm congratulated him heartily for the "the splendid work you have done in creating enthusiasm for the mountains among Canadians." He concluded: "I have never experienced anything like the kindness and hospitality shown me by everybody and above all by Mrs. Wheeler and yourself." They also contributed handsomely to the clubhouse building fund.

Clara had been at camp and, with her father, travelled on the special train to Victoria. At seventy-seven, Professor Macoun's zest and energy were undiminished. He had spent the summer collecting on Vancouver Island, and undoubtedly the visiting scientists found that the tour he led through Vancouver's Stanley Park was a very spirited one.

Clara remained for some time at the Coast where she received a letter from Mrs. Solly, expressing thanks "for all your goodness to us and for giving us such a perfectly delightful time; we hadn't imagined anything half so charming.... I know it must have taken a great deal of thought and arranging beforehand for everything to work so smoothly.... I couldn't help feeling we were wearing you out...." Mrs. Benson wrote: "When we parted from Mr. Wheeler at Glacier House we just felt the show was over! If we had journeyed only to the Winnipeg meetings it would have been a poor trip, but the three weeks in the mountains we will never forget.... Your Father was so surrounded by all the Botany folk on the train that we poor folk who know not Botany got scarcely a word with him.... His car was by far the gayest on the homeward journey! We do hope your Victoria visit is doing you good and that you are getting stronger."

Clara inherited her parents' strength of character but not their physical stamina. At forty-six her health began to cause serious concern; as their silver wedding anniversary drew near it was one of the circumstances which brought significant change to their lives. She returned from her rest at Victoria in late November and journeyed almost immediately to Ottawa where Arthur joined her in time for the marriage of her youngest sister, Nellie, early in January.

Ever since the initial refusal of the Minister of the Interior to allow him time off to superintend the Club camp that year, Wheeler had reason to assume that he would be faced with a vital decision affecting his career. The Minister had reacted to pressure but specified that Wheeler's leave was only for the important 1909 camp. Wheeler took action to meet the contingency should it arise.

Late in the year and early in 1910 he met with Club executive members; they made an important revision of the constitution providing for the appointment of a Managing Director for the Club. The appointment was subject to ratification by members at the summer Annual Meeting. And he took further steps in Ottawa. Arranging for "a deputation from the Alpine Club of Canada to wait upon the Minister", he drafted a statement stressing the important national role of the Club; he wired Professor Coleman and other influential eastern members who came to present the statement to Mr. Oliver. He was bitterly disappointed when he wrote in his diary: "Delegation all briefed. No results."

He went on his annual lecture tour, addressing the Montreal, Toronto, Ottawa, and Winnipeg Canadian Clubs on "Our Mountain Heritage" and early in February was back in his Calgary office attending to the map work with his men and writing his report of the previous season's surveys. The maps classified land suitable for orchards, farming, grazing, and timber resources; reports provided detailed outlines of survey activities and included climatic conditions and professional observations about the potential for irrigation and increasing settlemement.

Clara had remained in the East and Arthur wrote to her every day; in sub-zero weather he took his usual early morning walk "along the hills above the Elbow" and enjoyed his social life. He even entertained at tea, with their housekeeper, "Miss Darke presiding"; his guests included the beloved Miss Mollison, who had befriended alpinists in her days as manageress of Mount Stephen House at Field and Glacier House, and the wives of Alpine Club members.

When Clara's letters referred to the fact that she "had been poorly again", their correspondence focussed on possible benefits she might derive from living in Victoria. On her return to Calgary early in April they "worked on plans for Clara's cottage at Sidney."

He had taken up the mapping of the Spillimacheen mountains—the group he longed to survey extensively—and in March, he had received a cable from the eminent British climber-explorer, Dr. T. G. Longstaff. Like his friend, Mumm, Longstaff had climbed in the Himalayas where he "attained the highest altitude yet made by man, 23,400 feet." On Mumm's enthusiastic recommendation he had decided to spend a season in the Rockies. Wheeler replied immediately, referring to the unexplored and tantalizing terrain lying south of the Spillimacheen River. Longstaff "at once fell in with the suggestions that we should endeavour to cross the range together and make a survey...." Wheeler had this prospect in mind as he prepared to send his men into the field as soon as the current season's survey instructions arrived.

When the document came it contained "no provision for Alpine Club work. Put in my resignation."

At fifty, after more than three decades of almost continuous work for the Department, it was not easy to sever connections and face an uncertain future.

As statesmen had taken tentative first steps toward the orderly incorporation of the North West, Wheeler, (like other pioneer surveyors), had played his role by surveying Indian reserves, laying out fledgling townsites along the railway which bound the Dominion from sea to sea. He had preceded settlers to stake out sections, townships, and roads where they could build new lives in a land of hope; he had located the necessary timber for railways and frontier buildings, and in his irrigation surveys he had played an important part in transforming thousands of acres of semi-arid land into fertile fields. Realizing a dream stirred by William Butler's moving descriptions of the Rocky Mountains, he had penetrated that mighty barrier and with his survey camera had begun to unlock the secrets of the high ranges.

When faced with the ultimatum to abandon work in what was for him a land of enchantment, he made his decision. The photo-topographical technique in which only a handful of surveyors had been trained was eminently well-suited for alpine mapping and he had considerable experience and tremendous enthusiasm for this branch of the profession.

Moreover, he would not be withdrawing his special service to his country. He felt he was nation building. By training young Canadians to climb he was developing citizens keenly concerned for the welfare of others. Climbing taught "patience, courage, strength of mind, intelligent foresight, perseverance and good temper—those qualities which make a nation in the highest sense." And he would continue to "awaken in Canadians an appreciation of their mountain heritage."

Wheeler's reaction to the federal government's refusal for assistance to the Club reveals interesting aspects of his character. In fact his response was strikingly similar to that of a seventeenth century Cuffe ancestor.

During one of the many tragic confrontations between Protestant and Roman Catholic partisans, the widow of Maurice Cuffe had a long lease on the lands and Castle Bally-rally. The armed native Irish (the Roman Catholic party) seized the property of Protestant neighbours and the Castle was besieged. Her landlord at last begged her to surrender. His request was refused with scorn. Instead she "'...desired the said Sir Valentine to assist us with some powthar for the better defense thereof....'"!

On receipt of the news that the Minister had terminated support of the Club, Wheeler immediately drafted a letter setting out his views and, with Mrs. Parker's ready collaboration, sent it for publication to "twenty-one principal newspapers in Canada." At the Annual Meeting the Club requested that the former government grant be tripled!

The seventeenth-century Mrs. Cuffe had made careful provisions for a sustained siege. Arthur Wheeler was acting decisively to secure his future.

In the summer of 1910 the Annual Meeting at camp in Consolation Valley appointed him "permanent Director of the Canadian Alpine Club at the highest salary" the organization could afford. He reminded members of the primary aim of the Club: to promote scientific study and exploration of Canadian alpine regions.

He was making preparations for two expeditions to advance this objective and provide "a fair sample of what we aspire to as if a life work...."

Chapter XI

As Wheeler began his spring whirlwind of activity at the Banff clubhouse and prepared for summer camp, Clara journeyed to Sidney. Probably she was concerned about her husband's unsettled future. On the train she was very ill and had to stop off at Glacier House. Nonetheless, at Sidney she bought a lot and arranged to have their house built.

When Oliver arrived at Banff in June, he was warmly congratulated by his father. He had graduated from Royal Military College, taking twelve of the thirteen prizes, including the Governor General's Gold Medal and the Sword of Honour. As usual he helped with camp preparation and activities.

An early arrival at camp was cordially greeted by Mr. Wheeler and immediately discovered "that work was the order of the day.... All tents had to be brushed...." The novice "went to work vigourously" but found it difficult to do a satisfactory job: "I found I was completely outclassed by a wiry little man of sunny temperament who managed to accomplish twice as much as I could... without any apparent need of rest.... This tireless individual was Dr. T. G. Longstaff, one of the most noted mountain climbers in the world."

Longstaff and his sister journeyed to Mount Assiniboine where he had the satisfaction of climbing the striking peak. It is interesting that although Wheeler had quarrelled bitterly with Jim Simpson, he nonetheless recommended him as trail guide and outfitter for the Longstaffs. On their return journey to Banff they met another eminent climber on his way to the mountain: A. Felix Wedgewood (a direct descendant of the famous English potter) who had climbed in the Andes. Bad weather foiled his attempt on the mountain but gained him a bride. The trio went on to the Club camp and a year later he and Miss Longstaff were married.

There was to be another romance arising from a friendship formed at that camp between Oliver and the Longstaffs, whom he took to Lake O'Hara; there they joined an expedition Wheeler had arranged, similar but on a more modest scale than the one in 1909. The Wheelers, Conrad Kain and Miss Vaux (a member of an eminent American Quaker family who had been visiting the Rockies for years, taking the earliest measurements of the Illecillewaet, Asulkan, Victoria and Wapta Glaciers) travelled by pack-train to Bow Lake.

Now a part of the Banff-Jasper scenic highway, it was then a faint trail in mountain solitudes, guarded by the rugged grandeur of the ranges which rise above the Bow River. Those were "halcyon days: ...green glades were starred with wildflowers, and on gravelled river islets bloomed in such vivid profusion that they looked like little rafts amid the racing green water."

At the lovely lake the horses were sent back and the climbers ascended Bow Glacier, crossed the névé below Nicholas Peak, and descended into Vulture Col. Conrad led one rope and Oliver the other, while Wheeler scouted ahead. All day the forlorn little crew were engulfed in a clammy "white and windy shroud" of mists. They thought they were lost. Oliver unroped and descended ahead of his shivering companions. Soon they heard his shout of triumph. He had found the pass. At dusk they reached and crossed Yoho Gacier, where ponies and "a comfy camp" awaited them. There was only a slight casualty. Wheeler had taken Miss Vaux "to see Gordon Canyon. Fell and hurt my ribs."

When his happy guests departed, he went to Sidney where he was "delighted with Clara's little house" and wandered about the tiny village. During the week of his visit Oliver arrived. This was the first time Clara had not been at camp and the gracious presence of the Director's "true helpmate and hostess" was sorely missed. The inner disquiet of that summer must have put a further strain on her health. She now had to face for an indefinite period the departure of her son. Oliver was leaving for England for further training with the Royal Engineers.

Leaving them together for a few more days, Wheeler hurried to his rendezvous with Longstaff at Golden. Conrad joined them with two packers, and Byron Harmon of Banff (whose excellent alpine photographs were already being extensively distributed) completed the party. Alpine Club members had been enthusiastic when Wheeler had outlined plans for exploring this area and had voted to contribute $450; Dr. Longstaff's contribution was an equal amount but this would barely cover expenses and salaries.

They set out on the Columbia on Captain Armstrong's old stern-wheeler and disembarked at Spillimacheen Landing. The pack-train met them and they followed along a faint miner's trail up Bugaboo Creek for fifteen miles. Then the trail completely disappeared. Conrad wrote to old friends: "Now I know what it is to be the first one through a new and unmarked valley." All wielded axes and saws to hack a way through fallen trees, "great giants" which at one point completely blocked the valley "where an avalanche had brought down a tremendous windfall." It took six days of hard labour to cover one stretch of twelve miles. They waded "waist deep from one side to the other of a rushing stream" to avoid the steep cliffs. To get the pack-train over a nine-thousand-foot pass, Mr. Harmon, Dr. Longstaff, and two packers had to rope up the horses: "...until one sees it, it is impossible to believe what the horses must do."

But Wheeler and Conrad managed to lug their survey equipment to ten stations at altitudes between seven and nine thousand feet where Wheeler was elated by a panorama of "magnificent snow-crests, innumerable glaciers, rock spires, snow peaks, a galaxy of snow, ice and rock." These were "glorious days" in spite of chopping "horrid trail...and jolly wetting." Longstaff observed that "the labour of climbing several thousand feet through slippery undergrowth full of poisonous Devil's Club was extremely exhausting and I found cutting trail with Harmon and the men a much lighter job."

Harmon returned from an excursion one day and reported seeing a splendid glacier. Wheeler and Conrad saw this rugged spectacle later from a photographic station. For the first time mountaineers and explorers were seeing those "pinnacles and towers...like needles shooting toward the sky, their roots in the immense glacier"—the Bugaboo Spires, which were to challenge climbers for years. Conrad's frustration was extreme. Time wouldn't allow an attempt on the finest rock climbs he had seen in Canada's mountains.

Wheeler's plan was to "cross the Divide to the Duncan Valley and travel north to connect" his surveys with stations he had occupied in the Selkirks. But, as Longstaff wrote, "the country was really unknown, and the actual difficulties turned out to be far too formidable to render the scheme practical in the month at our disposal."

They had already been snowbound for a day and "the risk of being blockaded" by October snows was too great. The party separated—Longstaff and Harmon were guided by a trapper to the nearest route to civilization at Kootenay Lake, while Wheeler and Conrad retraced their steps with packers and horses. Conrad shot game to augment their meagre food supply, and on many an evening, sizzling bear steaks brightened campfires. On October 1st they were back at Spillimacheen. Conrad couldn't sleep—a bed with sheets was "too soft and comfortable"!

Shortly after his resignation from the Department, Wheeler had boldly proposed another expedition under the auspices of the Alpine Club. The Grand Trunk Pacific Railway was pushing its line through Yellowhead Pass west of Jasper and "virtually nothing was known of the region being opened up...." George Ryley, Wheeler's friend during his apprenticeship and early years with the Department, had been Land Commissioner and chief townsite agent for the Grand Trunk Pacific since 1905. Undoubtedly Wheeler's first proposal was addressed to him. Just before the 1910 camp Wheeler learned that his suggestion was being seriously considered.

His plan was to make a thorough exploration of the Mount Robson area. This fascinating region was not totally unknown to some Alpine Club members. Wheeler had read surveyor James McEvoy's 1898 report which indicated that Robson was probably the highest mountain in the Canadian Rockies. At the Club's founding meeting Wheeler had persuaded Professor Coleman and his brother that a first ascent of the peak would be an excellent inaugural feat, gaining world-wide attention for the Club. The Colemans were not overly enthusiastic.

When the C.P.R. was being built through the Selkirks, the Toronto professor had made his first attempt to reach what were then officially considered to be the highest mountains on the continent. Since fur-trading days, Mount Brown and Mount Hooker, flanking Athabasca Pass, had possessed this distinction on all available maps. During subsequent expeditions in search of the legendary mountains, the Colemans had blazed an important trail. But when they reached their mountains they found they were "frauds", being only a little over nine thousand feet in altitude, instead of between fifteen and seventeen thousand. In the light of this experience they were not about to set out on another arduous expedition in search of the reputedly superior peak. But Wheeler's persuasive powers were irresistible. This time the Colemans were not disappointed. Mount Robson was indeed Monarch of the Rockies.

In 1907, accompanied by an ardent young climber from Victoria, the Rev. George B. Kinney, the Colemans made a gallant attempt to capture the peak. But weeks of bad weather turned them back, and it foiled their dogged effort the next year. Kinney made one last perilous but futile solo attempt. They arranged to return in 1909. But before the Colemans could leave, in early spring, Kinney heard that a party of "foreigners" were coming to climb Mount Robson. Against all odds, he started out alone from Edmonton.

Near Jasper he encountered a young newcomer. Although Curly Phillips had never climbed a mountain in his life, Kinney persuaded him to attempt the formidable peak! On their return journey they met the "foreigners" on their way in. Kinney proudly announced that they had climbed the mountain. The "foreigners" were none other than Mumm, Hastings, and Amery.

Examining Robson's snowy heights, Mumm's guide, Inderbinen, confidently proclaimed that the summit would be theirs in eight hours. It was not; and they missed death by inches on its treacherous upper cliffs before abandoning the attempt. Late in 1909 Wheeler rejoiced when he heard from Kinney that his Robson climb had been crowned with victory.

But Wheeler's 1911 expedition was to be more ambitious. In keeping with the purpose of the Club to increase scientific knowledge of the mountains, he was determined to supplement the survey-exploration with geological, zoological, and botanical studies. In a spirit of nationalism he "earnestly tried" to enlist Canadian scientific backing, approaching the Director of the Geological Survey through Professors Macoun and Coleman. He was unsuccessful. He then appealed to his personal friend, geologist, Dr. Charles Walcott, Secretary of the Smithsonian Institute, who had been a visitor to the Rockies for years. Walcott "took the matter up with enthusiasm." Mr. Ned Hollister, Assistant Curator of Mammals at the United States National Museum, came to collect; Mr. Riley from the Museum collected birds, and with two assistants they subsequently took home "over nine hundred specimens and a plant collection of two hundred species."

Wheeler was still at work encouraging the greatest possible support for the Robson work when he returned from Banff to Sidney late in October. The expedition promised to be an exciting beginning for the life's work he had charted, but there still remained the need to earn a living. He soon learned that the Director's salary (a motion he doubtless persuaded the Executive to present to the members with full confidence that it would be ratified) would not be forthcoming as it would over-extend the Club's resources.

During his August visit he had informed the government of British Columbia that he was available for survey work. Characteristically, he didn't see the lower echelons of the civil service and fill out application forms. He called on the Lieutenant Governor, Premier, Surveyor General, and the Minister of Public Works. In October he called again, urging collaboration for the Robson expedition. A suggestion that the program could include surveying and monumenting the boundary between Alberta and British Columbia at Yellowhead Pass was discussed. This would be the first step in the long task of surveying the inter-provincial boundary. If—and it seems probable—it was Wheeler who first broached the subject, it was an astute move.

The immediate professional outlook was promising, and before Christmas he dashed back to Calgary to persuade two younger associates, R. D. McCaw and A. J. Campbell to join his private practice at the Coast.

Western Canada was in the midst of a railway construction boom. Since the 1890s there had been a settlement at Bella Coola and the isolated community had vainly petitioned for improved transportation. Two British railway and colonization companies had plans for building a line into the interior; surveys for the townsite, waterfront, and rail line were needed and land had to be staked for the expected settlers. Wheeler was successful in securing a very substantial contract including a large subdivision at Tetachuck Lake, about seventy-five miles northeast of Bella Coola, and in 1912, a contract for the townsite.

Clara had been very ill just before he left early in February to make a brief preliminary assessment of the nature of the work at Tetachuck Lake. Travelling by steamer past the heavily timbered inlets which bite into the rugged coastline, he completed his work, and on May 2nd, McCaw and Campbell took the outfit into the field. By the end of the month the work was well in hand and, deeply concerned about Clara, he left his partners with detailed instructions and returned to Sidney.

When he went back to the field in October, the party had worked their way one hundred and fifty miles from Bella Coola. He was delighted with the "good suppers, snug camps, good brush beds and fine mulligan for breakfast." Going over the season's work he found the surveyed meadows "more extensive than expected", and examined facilities for "a dam at Tetachuck Lake". He was satisfied that the "men had done good work". That was praise indeed from their demanding chief! In cold and snow they made an uncomfortable and arduous journey back to Bella Coola and the steamer.

At home he took up the usual chores required of the man of the house in those days. First came the satisfying task of "making good fires", and their replenishment meant many afternoon hours with saw and axe to stock the wood pile. Often rising at 4:30, he worked in his office on reports, maps, voluminous correspondence, press releases, and editorial work for the *Canadian Alpine Journal.*

By the time he wrote his report for the *Journal* that year, he was able to announce the successful completion of all negotiations and plans for the Robson expedition, which was to be "under my personal direction and the auspices of the Alpine Club of Canada." The British Columbia government had contributed $1,000 for the surveying and mapping, and the Alberta and federal governments had each granted another $500 for the Club's work. Not only had the Grand Trunk Pacific responded most generously to his request for $2,500, but he was also "armed with a letter from President Hays that will make matters very easy while in the sphere of influence of that Railway."

He referred also to the time when he had had to choose between development of the Club and his career with the Department: "...a cataclysm that seemed at the time to leave us little this side of the grave. Today we are able to laugh at so trifling a disturbance, and to proceed on our way, impelled by the great force behind us, which, like the rivers of ice that flow from the midst of the glorious alpine regions, is slow and silent, but irresistible." The remarks refer to the vicissitudes of the Club, but consciously or not, they reflect his response to life's vital problems.

It was also a pleasure to announce that Mrs. Wheeler would be at camp "to superintend arrangements." Mrs. Pat Burns, the wife of Calgary's meat-packing tycoon, had taken her place the previous year. Perhaps because

Clara's bouts of illness increased gradually over the years, he had become resigned to her condition, or, blessed with sturdy good health himself, he may have persuaded himself to take the optimistic view that her failing health was only of a temporary nature. Because she always rallied and resumed her activities he may not have been aware, as her good friend Mrs. Parker was, that this was "a continual triumph over physical frailty.... She suffered much, but who ever heard a whimper?"

As soon as he had his men in the field at Bella Coola in May, preparations began for the busy and exciting summer. By mid-June he and Clara were bound for Banff. Again, she had to stop overnight at Glacier House. She was "very sick". But she was at the clubhouse opening, which bustled with the arrival of guests. At the end of the month she and Arthur parted at Calgary, where she began "dismantling the house".

With Conrad Kain and the Rev. Mr. Kinney, Wheeler left for his rendezvous with the Grand Trunk Pacific dignitaries on their special train at Edmonton. In less than a year he was off on a second expedition into "virtually unknown alpine regions".

Chapter XII

The tiny settlement of Jasper had enjoyed a long solitude since the days when it had been on the main fur-trade route to the Pacific. Henry Moberly had been in charge of the little Hudson's Bay Company post during part of that era and a number of native families bear his name. That member of Collingwood's distinguished family had married one of the comely natives of the mountain wilderness.

Now it was being awakened by the bustle and activity of the railway builders. The Grand Trunk Pacific was making plans to exploit its alpine scenery by building a splendid hotel to rival the C.P.R.'s Banff Springs Hotel, and one of Wheeler's first services to the Company was to assist its officials in the selection of a site. Fiddle Creek seemed ideal. "In beautiful park-like land, set with spruce and graceful waving aspens...ablaze with glorious orange lilies, white and pink orchids, wild roses, yellow gallardias, the hotel will command a magnificent view of snow-clad peaks, grassy hills, dark green forest, rushing torrents and shining lakes....Here at this eastern entrance to Nature's Wonderland...visitors can pause luxuriously...to prepare for the enthralling scenes that lie beyond the massive portal." The mineral waters from Miette Hot Springs were to be piped down to the hotel.

From Fiddle Creek a construction engine and caboose took Wheeler and the G.T.P. officials to the end of steel at a bridge over the Creek. In seconds catastrophe threatened. The engine broke through the bridge and plunged into the creek. Miraculously, the engineer and fireman escaped with only minor injuries and the caboose stayed on the track.

At Edson, Wheeler had sent the main pack-train ahead along the railway tote road to Yellowhead Pass. It was in charge of the very able packer and guide, Curly Phillips, who had climbed on Robson with Kinney.

Fred Stephens, Professor Norman Collie's beloved guide and companion, had accompanied Mumm and the Professor on their exploring and climbing expeditions to Robson and northward for two years. Now he was to take Wheeler to Phillips's camp up the Yellowhead. Almost immediately there was trouble and Wheeler's temper flared. "Fred Stephens would be damned if he would pack in the rain." Stephens was accustomed to Collie's less tempestuous manner; Wheeler would never tolerate dallying in the field, especially for such a trifle as rain! Certainly he was not in the habit of having orders contradicted. Stephens calmly announced that he was in charge of the pack train and Wheeler had to cool his heels until mid-afternoon.

His irritation subsided as they rode toward Jasper townsite. In the south the superb snowy wedge of today's Mount Edith Cavell towered serenely, and in the blue, misty distance the Athabasca "opened vistas of deep gorges...rugged peaks and castellated towers of rock, capped by snow where clouds swirled and wreathed round their crests."

Turning west up the Miette River, they travelled on "the miserable wagon road." Mules strained with loads of freight and labourers carrying packs made their way between railway work camps. Wheeler wanted to press on to overtake Phillips as quickly as possible but Stephens insisted on camping "in a dirty littered site"; their supper consisted of crackers, sardines, and jam. Stephens was getting even. It was a further unaccustomed indignity to start next morning "without soap or breakfast". Wheeler was always fastidious in camp—his nightshirt and linen were laundered, even when, in the early days, this meant taking them out some distance to a farmer's wife.

At Yellowhead summit they camped at a railway contractor's camp. "The place was tough and rowdy...there was a shooting there that night but no one seemed hurt." Their next stop, on the Moose River, was equally disagreeable. At "Moose City" Conrad had his clothes stolen; "slick thieves also made off with a considerable quantity of grub", and their stove was "abstracted" to appear that night as a stake in a poker game. "However in this section one learns to accept trifles of this kind with true philosophy, which in our case meant buying another stove at twice the price."

They left the construction sites thankfully and made their way toward Robson amid the beauty and solitude of the Moose River Country. But "the going was bad...horses floundered in muskegs...much to the detriment of the packs and most trying to the temper of the packers. At times like this the atmosphere is usually sulphurous, but Phillips refrained and wore his imperturbable smile...."

Following Resplendent Creek, they established camp and "the business of the expedition now began in earnest." The American scientists set off to hunt in the numerous side valleys and the topographic party took "a flying camp outfit to explore the head of Reef Glacier and valley."

Conrad had been hired to select the best route and act as guide to the camera stations. One of Wheeler's first objectives was a high peak in the Lynx Range and at once he differed with Conrad's choice of route. "Conrad deferred to my views." Ascending "a rock wall [which] rose very steeply for 1500 feet" gave some good climbing but they narrowly missed "being buried by an avalanche." They realized the light wouldn't be suitable for photographing if they continued to the summit, so Wheeler had to do his camera work on a ridge below.

Conrad had been right, but Wheeler wouldn't admit it. The easy-going Kain could accept the master-servant attitude which Wheeler often demanded. With others, equally self-willed, fiery encounters were the order of the day. In some cases this meant life-long bitterness. But not on Wheeler's part. Once the storm was over he would assume that geniality would be restored and very often it was. However, all irritations were forgotten when they approached their goal.

*Mount Robson, focal point of Wheeler's 1911
expedition.*

"As we topped the crest the whole wonderful panorama came into
view. At our feet flowed the Robson Glacier.... Across the wide river of
ice...the great massif of Robson, rising supreme above all other peaks. White
against a sky of perfect blue, it seemed to belong to a world other than our
own." Ethereal, snowy Mount Resplendent, crowned with immense sculptured
cornices; the splendid sharp conical peak of Mount Whitehorn; "...it was the
most stupendous alpine scene I had ever gazed upon, setting the blood coursing
through the veins as fast as a torrent, with the pure joy of being alive—and
there."

There was absolutely no doubt about it: "these peaks will provide
excellent work when we hold our annual camp at the summit of Robson
Pass."

At this station they were on the watershed, the boundary between
Alberta and British Columbia. Next day, ascending to a low peak on the east
ridge of Lynx Mountain, they were crossing "a slope of ice covered by new
snow." Wheeler was following in Conrad's footsteps, and as there was no
difficulty they were not roped. "Suddenly the footsteps broke away and I slid
down the slope to where it ended abruptly." In his wake the ice axe scraped
uselessly on the ice.

"I had made up my mind that it was the end." Suddenly he stopped. His axe had caught. "There was not however much to spare, for the lower half of my body was over the edge...." Vacant space yawned between his dangling legs and the rocks below. Conrad leapt down the slope "in reckless bounds, a look of horror in his eyes....He grabbed my shoulder and gasped, 'I've got you!' And then he began to slide. My axe held and we were soon on our feet." Conrad had acted with "tremendous daring, much presence of mind and great disregard of the consequences to himself."

The shock of such a fall would be very serious to a man of fifty-one, but Wheeler was in excellent physical condition. He soon pulled himself together and in spite of a very sore right arm continued to "Reef Glacier station" to work.

He wrote that "there are some for whom a knife edge in the air has no terrors. I am not one of these; I climb in fear and trembling, fully knowing the result of a slip or weakening of the physical powers. But it is worth it....To feel the thrill of danger and the tingle of the keen rarified air. To see the whole world and glory of it!...I know of no more fascinating avocation than the disentangling of Nature's puzzle in the breaking up of the original terrain and the reducing of it to a readable map."

Camp was moved within sight of a "fine-looking peak" which Wheeler christened "The Colonel", "after Col. Ami Laussedat, a French scientist who first brought to public notice the method of making topographical surveys by means of photography." To reach the peak, they crossed alpine meadows which were "literally covered with purple asters, wild geraniums, Indian Paint Brush, scarlet and yellow columbines, forget-me-nots and pink and white heath and heather." After an easy climb to the 9,166-foot summit they were amply rewarded. It was fitting that from the mountain named for the "Father of photo-topographical surveying" the Great Divide could be readily traced for miles. That watershed was soon to be mapped by the Colonel's technique.

"The immensity of the view is astounding—the immeasurable chaos of it all! It will take years before it can be sorted out and set in order." A very accurate assessment.

They needed a raft to cross Moose River. Conrad was "a grand climber and a magnificent guide under all conditions" and, Wheeler observed, "he will attempt anything." He built his first raft but "was much chagrined" to find it would carry only one passenger instead of the three who had to cross. Phillips, "a river man of such skill that he can cross any kind of water on a single stick big enough to hold him," set out, taking one end of a climbing rope to fasten to a tree on the other shore. Attaching the raft to the fixed rope with a stout loop, he quickly pulled himself back. Assuming all was well, he disappeared with his gun up the hill after some goats, missing the ensuing "circus".

"The impromptu ferry" was hauled up, and shouldering his transit, Wheeler crossed, but when he reached the swift water near the shore the boiling current bore down on the front end of the craft until "it hung absolutely vertical." He was pitched into the icy water. Encumbered with his instrument and impeded by his injured and partially disabled right arm, he "couldn't make it up the steep part of the rope" fastened to the tree. "I kicked out like a steer and yelled that I couldn't get out." Conrad frantically brought the raft back but when he arrived, he also slid off the vertical craft! Wheeler managed to reach a tree on shore and Conrad, swimming strongly, helped him out. The ferry was improved by fastening it with two ropes and Kinney, carrying his camera, crossed safely.

They continued their explorations and photography to Moose Pass, Calumet Creek, and, early in August, camped at Robson Pass. As they ate breakfast they looked at Mount Robson, silhouetted against the blue-black sky; the palette of the rising sun shaded the summit snow with delicate pink, brushed a straight black band across it, and flushed the cliffs beneath with deep rose which slowly blazed into gold, and faded into silver.

At Berg Lake camp they heard the sound "like the report of cannon" as immense blocks of ice broke from the icefield to rattle down the steep incline into the lake. On impact, spouts of water leapt twenty feet into the air.

They climbed a mountain to view the Robson Glacier, where Conrad picked out what he claimed to be "the proper route of ascent." It was the route attempted by Mumm and his party in 1909. Certainly Conrad longed to make an attempt on the famous peak and some Alpine Club members later condemned Wheeler for not allowing him to make the ascent. Perhaps they are right and Wheeler did so in order to have the Alpine Club reap the glory when they came to camp there. But equal consideration should be given to Wheeler's justification of his actions: theirs was not a mountaineering expedition but a topographical one. There was work to be done and the Robson area is notorious for brewing storms.

From another vantage point Conrad confirmed his previous selection of route. Wheeler was skeptical of Conrad's estimate "that the climb could be made in eight hours...but, of course, Conrad is a wonder!...I should like to have made an attempt to verify Conrad's statement and my assistants would have been nothing loth...."

Indeed, his climbing assistants were keen for a try! Kinney had his own private reason for wanting to go on the mountain again—a secret which only leaked out to a few climbers within a year.

Conrad's frustration was unbearable. Here he was, surrounded by virgin summits and no opportunity to meet their challenges! When the party was unable to work because of fog and rain, and descended from their high camp, Conrad was "overcome by ennui". He wandered off to climb Mount Whitehorn.

Both he and Wheeler had agreed that this 11,100-foot peak would make "a splendid and difficult climb". When he reached a high ridge a thunderstorm struck and he almost turned back. But, doggedly, he struggled upward to the summit. There were no rocks to build a cairn, so he descended a short distance from the snowy apex and "made a little stone man". On a slip of paper he wrote his name and date and enclosed it in a metal match holder with "N. Hollister" scratched on the side. He carefully put this inside the cairn for he "knew that people would not believe I had reached the summit." It was only later that he realized that it was his twenty-eighth birthday.

The descent was perilous. Nightfall overtook him on the glacier. Greatly tempted to spend the night there, he resisted: "in five minutes I would have been frozen stiff from head to foot." A fearsome thunderstorm saved him: the lightning flashes helped him avoid the gaping crevasses. When at last he reached the rocks, he "yodelled with delight". In pouring rain he arrived at camp before daybreak and crawled quietly into bed.

Wheeler had been extremely anxious when he hadn't returned at night; he kept up a blazing fire as a beacon and fired rifles in case he was lost. He received the announcement of his guide's achievement with mixed feelings. He was relieved and proud, but would not accept the feat as "an official first ascent." Knowing Conrad, he had "complete confidence in his word", but believed that the account of his lone attempt could never be verified. Without doubt he was also angry that Conrad had risked such danger. Conrad himself admitted that "it was one of the craziest and most foolhardy undertakings that I ever made in the mountains..."

Two years later climbers returned from Whitehorn with Conrad's metal container and its enclosure. He was vindicated but rather indifferent about it. He knew he had climbed the mountain and all his life he would "remember the ascent of Whitehorn." As well, he had just returned from a more treasured victory.

In 1911 Wheeler and Conrad looked with glasses at Robson's steep west and south-west face as Kinney pointed out the route of his 1909 climb with Phillips. Wheeler marvelled not only at the wonder of the ascent, but "the wonder of their ever having made the descent without accident."

They continued their work, climbing, riding, and tramping from valley to valley, "each more beautiful than the last." Their camps (except where the ubiquitous mosquitoes were vicious) were all "a joy to those who delight in Nature....Rare and delicate alpine blossoms are your carpet, heath and heather grow in your tent, where you sleep on fragrant balsam brush that out-rivals the best of mattresses."

Even the fact that their food supply was often down to cornmeal and goat meat failed to dampen Wheeler's enjoyment: "I know of no more revivifying tonic after a hard day's climbing than a bowl of goat soup." The cook may have excelled in this specialty but he consistently burned the porridge. When his chief grumbled his dissatisfaction, he blamed it on a faulty pot. Wheeler volunteered to prove this was not so. Next morning he sat over the fire outside the tent, carefully stirring porridge. Inside, Conrad, the incomparable raconteur, regaled his companions with a tale concocted on the spot. The chef *pro tem* became engrossed in the story. Once more they had burned porridge.

Near the end of August they were completing the last sections of work in the Robson area and Wheeler was examining sites for the proposed Grand Trunk Pacific chalets. On August 23rd a messenger came looking for him with a packet of mail. It contained a letter from Alpine Club President Patterson with news of "Clara's sudden seizure and subsequent illness."

He immediately wired the Club's devoted Executive Secretary, Mr. Mitchell, inquiring "where and how Clara was." Numb with shock and worry, he plodded on with his work. Sick with "grippe", he ached in every bone and "could scarcely drag my legs along." But the work had to be finished, for the season was drawing to a close.Two days later he got Mitchell's wire about Clara: "Very reassuring, and relieving me of much anxiety."

Her "grave illness" had struck at Lake Louise Chalet and she was taken to the Banff hospital as soon as possible. After many weeks she won "her gallant fight for life"—a victory which Mrs. Parker believed belonged as much to the "triumph of her spirit" as it did to the doctors who cared for her. Undoubtedly her responsibilities as Club hostess precipitated the heart attack, but her doctors advised her not to return to the high altitudes which they considered a danger to anyone in her condition.

Early in September, Wheeler's expedition had completed the first circuit of Mount Robson, having travelled eighty-five miles and climbed peaks from seven to eleven thousand feet high. He made the first topographical survey within that area and produced the first map. On September third, after ascertaining the summit of Yellowhead Pass, a cairn was built and inscribed. It was the first monument marking the Alberta-British Columbia boundary.

The party then made their way to that gem of the Canadian Rockies, Maligne Lake. "It was a perfect afternoon when I came to the Lake. In its setting of towering peaks, forests of golden-green and dark blue-green spruce it was incomparable...."

He had little time but "climbs enabled the Lake to be mapped with a fair degree of accuracy." And the vistas from the heights! The narrow far-reaching valleys of the Sunwapta and Whirlpool; barely discernible, noble Mount Columbia rising from its massive icefield; "the gigantic fangs" of the Tonquin valley—all "called the explorer with no uncertain voice."

There were no qualifications about his recommendation that the boundary of Jasper Park must be extended to include Maligne Lake and he selected a site for a chalet. The lovely lakes near the railway in the Athabasca Valley "must be stocked with fish." And at Maligne "all destruction of big game must be absolutely prohibited...preserving them in their native habitat will prove of infinitely greater value to the country than to advertise them as spoils of the chase." Trails must be built to connect valley to valley so travellers can escape "the turmoil of cities to renew health and spirit amidst these snow-clad mountains."

Byron Harmon continued to take the first beautiful photographs of the Jasper, Robson and Maligne area. As he, Conrad, and Curly Phillips were now going on a remarkable journey, he could add to his collection which contains some of the finest alpine photography.

Wheeler longed to accompany them but had other obligations to meet. In mid-September, as snow began to fall, he sent them off with instructions to make careful observations about the feasibility of constructing a pony trail from Jasper to Lake Louise. They were to note grades, zig zags, blastings, and bridging required. With horses wallowing in deep snow on high passes, they made "the 120 mile journey" to Lake Louise station in eleven days along what is now the scenic Jasper-Banff highway.

In two and a half months Wheeler had occupied thirty-six stations in the Jasper, Robson, and Maligne area. He reported that "...the expedition was no picnic or pleasurable excursion....When I look back on some of those climbs...where Konrad guided me...the almost perpendicular snow slopes down which we frequently made a path, I feel thankful that it is over for the present. And yet I would do it all again to behold the glories."

The work of the Smithsonian Institute made headlines in Washington papers, and early in 1912 Wheeler was lecturing to Canadian Clubs about the beauties of the Yellowhead country and preparing "interviews for the press". His enthusiasm influenced the British Columbia government's decision to create Mount Robson Provincial Park and his articles appeared in American and European alpine and geographical journals.

Chapter XIII

When Wheeler returned to Victoria, Clara was better—there is no mention of her illness. She had a circle of friends and Surveyor General Dawson became a mutual friend with whom they dined at the very grand Empress Hotel. Wheeler found the aristocratic atmosphere particularly congenial, often taking tea there with lady companions.

His survey business thrived; in addition to the Bella Coola townsite subdivision, his men worked on the Gulf Islands. A member of the Legislature had made an exploratory expedition which led to the establishment of Strathcona Park on Vancouver Island, an area almost unknown and inaccessible. Local branches of the Alpine Club had been formed in most major Canadian centres and the Vancouver Island section planned an excursion to this beautiful spot. Wheeler's climber friend, W. W. Foster, Deputy Minister of Public Works, had given Wheeler's firm a contract to survey the road from Alberni to Long Beach.

He also had plans for a Club camp at Mount Robson. Just before leaving for his eastern tour he received disquieting news which provided added impetus to this project.

It is intriguing to speculate about how the news reached Club officials. Wheeler's first letter came from Club President Patterson of Toronto. He reported that Rev. Mr. Kinney had not reached the actual summit of Mount Robson. Dr. Coleman and Mumm also conveyed the news to the Club Director.

When Conrad, Harmon, Kinney, and Phillips ended their Maligne to Banff journey, Conrad returned with Phillips to spend the winter trapping in the Jasper area. During those days of isolation, Phillips undoubtedly shared his secret. He and Kinney had reached a point within a few yards of the summit in bad weather and it was too dangerous to complete the ascent. It is very probable that Kinney would never have claimed complete victory if he had not been sorely tempted when he met "the foreigners"—undoubtedly he thought the news would turn them back.

Conrad considered their feat remarkable, but would have been reluctant to have it falsely recorded as an official first ascent of the great peak. He *may* have been the first to write Wheeler about the incident, but this is doubtful. It would be difficult for Wheeler to accept the fact that a man of the cloth, a class traditionally held in the highest esteem by Wheelers, could perpetuate such a deception. More likely Conrad broke the news to some of his good friends in the English Club. Wheeler and Club officials discussed the matter and one senses that Wheeler's views as to the best solution prevailed: a crack Canadian team under the auspices of the Club must make the ascent and remain discreetly quiet about the previous claim to avoid unfavourable publicity. Immediately he went to work soliciting the necessary public support and that of the G.T.P. for the Robson camp in 1913.

On his way home from his lecture tour he bought Clara "a bracelet from Birks" and they had a quiet reunion at the Empress. In Sidney she had been supervising "an addition to the house". Actually, it was an annex which was to be her parents' last home. A stroke had left eighty-year-old Professor Macoun with a disabled right hand but he learned to use his left hand and continued an active life, collecting and writing. They arrived "all in good shape", accompanied by their eldest son James and a nurse who would live with them.

Someone had to assume Clara's duties at the clubhouse and camp. In April, Club Secretary Mitchell invited Wheeler to meet the applicant he considered suitable. Their good friend, Miss Mollison joined them for the interview—her long experience as hostess would be helpful in judging the young lady's qualifications.

Miss Emmeline Savatard was the daughter of the Reverend Louis Savatard, Vicar of Holy Trinity Church, Darawen, Lancashire. Trained as a dietitian at Liverpool College, she emigrated to Canada with her two sisters. At thirty-two she was shorter and not as slender as Clara; her facial features were less finely drawn; a very prominent, firm jaw-line suggests strength of will, and a fresh complexion and beautiful blue eyes enhanced a very pleasing appearance.

On June 9th she went with Wheeler and Mitchell to Banff and was installed as "chatelaine of the clubhouse", where Wheeler began the office work of his survey business and made preparations for camp to be held at Vermilion Pass.

Construction had begun on the first highway across the main chain of the Rockies at this pass, and on the trek to camp ladies with parasols and long gowns trailing in the dust picked their way round the boulders left by dynamite blasts. A masculine novice appreciated the "warm hand-shake from that benevolent despot, the Camp Director," who, he soon discovered, was "the male counterpart of the famous 'She Who Must be Obeyed'.... I have heard whispers that those who failed to keep to camp rules had to take their sticks and depart.... But joking apart, Mr. Wheeler is father and friend to all in camp. To see him of a morning planted upon as sturdy a pair of legs as ever trod a mountain side, while the climbing parties...file out before him, to hear the terse, vigourous advice and encouragement...is to realize that we have to do with a man who knows how to handle men."

With his genial sense of humour (and vanity) Wheeler appreciated these comments. Mrs. Julia Henshaw, a writer from Vancouver who photographed mountain flora with great skill, took a photograph of him which he included in the *Canadian Alpine Journal.* As editor, he chose the caption: "He Who Must be Obeyed".

Mrs. Henshaw had caught him in a casual pose beside a mountain stream: smiling, leaning on his ice-axe, wearing breeches and well-cut Norfolk

"He Who Must Be Obeyed."

jacket, inconspicuous neckerchief, puttees, stout boots, soft, creased fedora set at a jaunty angle, neat moustache and beard, slightly greying sideburns—at fifty-two the Wheeler charm was still very evident.

Oliver returned from England on leave that summer and the hospitable Sidney home was filled with happily re-united Wheelers and Macouns. James Macoun, biologist with the Geological Survey (where he was carrying on his father's work), and William, a horticulturalist at the Experimental Farm at Ottawa, came for working holidays. They accompanied the Vancouver Island section of the Alpine Club on its excursion to Strathcona Park. Oliver led a party to the summit of Mount Elkhorn where, in Wheeler's words, they "gave three cheers for the Alpine Club of Canada, for our leader, my son, and the magnificent new Alpine fields as yet unconquered..."

At the end of the summer Arthur and Clara saw Oliver off on the boat. His departure must have been a poignant experience. Their twenty-two year-old soldier-engineer would not only be gone for an indefinite period—he was going to a strange, remote, and exotic land.

Oliver probably decided to pursue his career in India for several reasons: adventure, which had lured Wheelers for generations, service to Empire, and perhaps most compelling, the possibility of penetrating the Himalayas. As he sailed for the land where he would build a career crowned with distinction, his father began his most satisfying and important contribution as a pioneer Canadian surveyor. In October he had an interview with the Surveyor General of British Columbia. "Very satisfactory." Indeed it was!

It assured him that the remaining years of his professional life would be spent in the Rockies he loved, doing work for which he was very well qualified, on a project to which he was passionately devoted: the advancement of scientific knowledge of Canada's mountains. For more than seven hundred miles it would take him from peak to peak—often to "alpine fields as yet unconquered"—to trace and record with instrument and practiced eye the ridgepole of the continent. It called for a family celebration: a champagne dinner at the Empress Hotel.

He had been appointed the British Columbia Commissioner of the three-member Interprovincial Boundary Commission which was to survey and map the Alberta-British Columbia border.

The barrier of mountains between the two provinces had been created in eons past when Earth's pent-up stresses had thrust up the rocky crest of the continental watershed. Before Confederation it was defined as the crest of the watershed of the Rocky Mountains and until 1913 there had been no need for more precise delineation. But as settlement crept nearer, as mining and timber resources began to be exploited, as more roads and railways were built, the line needed to be defined for administrative purposes.

Giving some support to the likelihood that Wheeler himself may have added impetus to the decision to proceed, is the fact that "in April 1912, the matter was taken up between the Surveyor General of Dominion Lands and the Surveyor General of British Columbia," at the instigation of the Minister of Lands for British Columbia. It may of course be a coincidence that this was shortly after Wheeler had had extensive interviews with Premier McBride and his ministers.

In 1913 his physical and administrative capabilities were to be exercised to the limit. In addition to the usual editing of the *Canadian Alpine Journal,* supervising his surveying office where the Maligne map was being prepared, his Director's responsibilities at the camp and clubhouse, there was also the need to organize and solicit support from the Grand Trunk Pacific for the Robson Camp. As well, he must get a team of good men into the field for the boundary survey working from Kicking Horse Pass to Assiniboine Pass. He had to occupy camera stations to delineate the watershed between these points and confer with his fellow commissioners at Crowsnest Pass.

While details of the survey instructions were being worked out by officials, he enjoyed the respite of hockey games in Victoria, nights at the theatre, and entertaining. The automobile age had arrived and people were "wheeling out" from town for tea. Hiring a driver and one of the shiny ornate vehicles of the day he took the family for drives, with "Granny Macoun" and Clara elegant in wide-brimmed hats and motoring veils. Frequently the wondrous machines stalled and the ladies had to walk home while gentlemen fiddled with the mysterious mechanical intricacies under the hood (usually without success) in attempts to get "the blame thing started".

He and Clara gardened with the enthusastic cooperation and advice of the Professor. Clara's bouts of illness limited her activities occasionally; she "was too poorly" to meet him when he returned from his trip East. She was unable to attend the annual banquet of the local Alpine Club so Miss Savatard accompanied him.

By late February, Commissioner for Alberta, R. W. Cautley, Commissioner for the Dominion, J. N. Wallace, and Wheeler had precise instructions from G. H.E. Deville, Surveyor General of Canada. The territory to be covered extended from "the International Boundary and the 120th degree of longitude and is the line dividing the waters flowing into the Pacific Ocean from those flowing elsewhere....This line may cross the meridian of 120th degree of longitude several times. Should this prove to be the case, the boundary shall follow the watershed line from the Boundary to the most northerly crossing of the meridian and thence follow the meridian to the 60th degree of latitude."

Cautley was to take levels and make the preliminary survey of the boundary in the passes and erect permanent monuments; his party was to consist of two chain men, one rodman, two axemen and monument builders, one cook, one packer and ten horses.

"The line survey must be made with great care." Those sections of the boundary traversed by passes would be the ones most frequently used, and often the watershed there is difficult to determine with precision. In addition, the monuments were to provide "a carefully measured base for the system of triangles on which the work of the topographical section of the Commission depends...."

When preliminary work had located the line, the Commissioners were to decide where the monuments would be placed. And it was imperative that the Commissioners agree on the placement of these monuments. They must "be on the actual watershed...and shall occupy naturally prominent positions...and wherever practicable, every monument must be visible from the next one." Trial lines were to be cut, the monuments built, a final survey executed, and then lines cut out between the monuments "so as to give a clear opening to the sky of six feet." Set on a two-foot concrete base, the twenty-inch zinc portion of the pyramidal monument was painted a bright red (visible in snow and timber) and brass identification plates affixed. The watershed is a sinuous one but in the passes it was to be marked as a "straight line survey" which was to be

A. O. Wheeler operates the camera on a high station.

extended to timberline, or above, on either side of the passes.

Wheeler's work was to survey the boundary beyond the passes: "a topographical delineation of the watershed by means of photo-topography.... The Boundary thus established is the natural watershed and is therefore not marked with monuments but it is capable of being mapped with greater accuracy than could possibly be attained in any other way..." His surveying and mapping was to extend several miles on each side of the boundary as well as the line extending above either side of the passes. At those high points his men erected cairns.

As these sites were inaccessible to horses Wheeler designed a lighter monument: a solid brass bolt with a four-inch shank was set in cement in a hole drilled in solid rock; over this a five to seven foot rock cairn was erected. "The weight of the sledge, drill, bolt and cement together with surveying instruments" made for back-breaking labour during difficult climbs for some of his party, which consisted of an assistant surveyor, two labourers, one cook, one packer, and ten horses.

Early in May he was at the clubhouse in his survey office and the Commissioners conferred there, completing plans for the season. He recruited men, and on May 29th they were sent into the field at Kicking Horse Pass in the charge of his assistant, Alan J. Campbell. S. H. Mitchell, the Club's Executive Secretary, took over the Director's administrative work at the clubhouse during his absence and acted as host. Wheeler hurried to Sidney to say good-bye to Clara, and when he came back to Banff, Miss Savatard had arrived to work there again. They went to Calgary where she shopped for clubhouse supplies and he for the survey and the O'Hara club camp. In the evening they relaxed at the theatre where *Peter Pan* was playing.

A flying visit to the field indicated that snow conditions would soon permit climbing, and on July 2nd Wheeler joined Campbell at Kicking Horse Pass. Thirty-one-year old Campbell had worked with Wheeler since 1909 but he had never been on a mountain. For the first year he was mortally afraid, certain that he would never be able to make the dangerous descent. Fortunately, that prince of guides, Conrad Kain, accompanied Wheeler, and under his patient and amiable tutelage, Campbell overcame his fear.

The first day's work on the shoulder of Mount Niblock was satisfactory; Wheeler repeated the ascent next day and bolt and cairn were erected: "Good climb. Got back in good shape." The station on the shoulder of Mount Bosworth was "very cold and disagreeable"; manipulating delicate instruments with numbed fingers, it took hours to precisely ascertain the watershed: "the apex of a narrow ridge" where they made their way along rock and ice crests to the 10,360-foot summit of Pope's Peak. Bolt and cairn were built on that summit and on that of Mount Bosworth, "which presents a forbidding and percipitious face...overlooking Bath Creek."

Campbell soon learned what was involved at these stations. Setting the transit-theodolite on its tripod, the time-consuming and patient "trigonometric levelling" began, "frequently entailing a precarious balancing over dizzy depths." Replacing the instrument with the camera, he saw "a chaos of mountains, snowfields, icefalls, forested valleys, streams, and lakes...a vast boundless ocean in a state of turmoil." Frequently a complete panoramic set "of views" was taken and the 6-1/2″ x 4-3/4″ glass plates had to be changed in a dark tent. Later, working patiently for months in the mapping office, hundreds of these plates were developed and enlarged, and from these the meticulous and gifted draughtsman, Alan S. Thomson, resolved the chaos seen on the peaks into an orderly array: "a map showing the various topographical features as a co-ordinate whole...."

Six brass bolts and cairns were erected at Kicking Horse Pass and seven camera stations occupied before the party was dispatched south to Vermilion Pass. Wheeler had "arranged for the program of work while I am at the Alpine Club Camps."

The first camp was situated near the imposing crags of Cathedral Mountain in the Kicking Horse Valley. Madly brushing tents, he "managed to keep ahead of the game" before the two hundred guests arrived. After camp, he and Gordon Cameron, a member of the survey crew, made the quick annual trip to measure the recession of the Yoho Glacier. Miss Savatard and two maids from the clubhouse accompanied them. "Glorious day; beds made under the trees; bothered at night by porcupine getting on Miss Savatard's bed." People crowded up to the clubhouse on their return and "Miss Savatard got lunch for them in short order".

Then he and Conrad set out for Edmonton to board the special G.T.P. train Wheeler had arranged for the Mount Robson camp. Sixty-nine active members enjoyed the memorable two weeks there. From Mount Robson siding they wandered in happy groups to Kinney Lake and up the cliffs to Berg Lake. It was a fifteen-mile walk along a track Curly Phillips had made (Wheeler had prompted the British Columbia government to pay the construction cost) but in the splendour of the alpine surroundings, weariness vanished. And at last the reward. In the words of an earlier visitor: "Cold, icy, clean-cut...Mount Robson, a noble, massive vision to the pilgrims who had come so far to seek her."

It was a pilgrimage for Conrad Kain, promising the greatest adventure of his life.

On the night of July 30th he, W. W. Foster, and A. H. MacCarthy of Summit, New Jersey, bivouaced high on the moraine along the route of ascent Conrad had chosen two years before. After a four o'clock breakfast they started up the glacier towards the cliffs uplifted in the cloudless sky. With skill, tenacity, and encouragement, he led his men ever upward; ice-slopes, walls of rock, a narrow snowy ridge ("with a splendid view into the depth below"), great overhanging cornices fringed with long icicles glittering in the sun—all were at last safety below them. Ahead towered walls of terraced snow, loose snow, where they sank to their hips. All about them lay virgin snow, wind-etched with "forms like ostrich feathers."

On a snow-ridge, "Conrad cut steps as though inspired." "Suddenly," he wrote, "I turned to my *Herren*. 'Gentlemen, that's as far as I can take you'."

A few more steps—and they were on the summit of Mount Robson. It was 5:30 p.m. The vertical view down to Berg Lake was "indescribably beautiful". Later, Conrad noted that they had only fifteen minutes on the pinnacle of the Monarch of the Rockies: "ten of pure pleasure and five of teeth chattering."

Descending by another route, Conrad took his men on the first traverse of the savage peak. He knew they must spend a night on the mountain but started off with a cheery, "I will find a way." At ten, they stopped on a narrow rock ledge, built a fragile rocky wall to protect them from the abyss below, and Conrad roped his *Herren* to a rock. As an avalanche roared nearby he observed, with unquenchable wit, "If that goes on, it will spoil my night's rest."

It was a long bone-chilling night at nine thousand feet.

At 6:30 the next morning the warm sun reached them. But MacCarthy and Foster were painfully snow-blind. Tenderly Conrad applied cold poultices to lessen the swelling and at last they could keep their eyes open.

At five in the afternoon they reached camp. With immense relief and a thrill of satisfaction, Wheeler greeted them. Others swarmed from the fire to join them. Adding to the glory were the warm congratulations of good friends and distinguished climbers, Mumm, Inderbinen, and the veteran of the Alpine Club, Professor Fay. Happily, too, the co-founder of the Club, Elizabeth Parker, was on hand to celebrate the great achievement made under the auspices of the Club and led by the Club's official guide.

All left that camp with nostalgic backward glances. Conrad left with a feeling of deep satisfaction that time and circumstance would never erase.

Chapter XIV

During Wheeler's absence, young Campbell had ably taken over his chief's duties at Vermilion Pass. On Wheeler's visit before leaving for camp, the boundary of the pass had been easily ascertained, and he and Cautley had agreed on monument sites. The camera stations were located and Campbell delineated the watershed and erected brass bolt monuments, the two highest on Boom and Storm mountains.

On August 20th, Wheeler and Conrad returned to work at Simpson Pass where Cautley and Campbell's parties were camped on the beautiful park-like summit. The tents were snugly set in groves of spruce and larch. Heather, and tiny lakes and winding streams made it one of those camps Wheeler loved.

Campbell was also in charge of Cautley's party. Travelling from Vermilion to Simpson Pass, his men had made their way over an almost non-existent trail in heavy rain. Fording the swollen Vermilion River, a pack horse lost its footing and was instantly carried downstream. All hands made a feverish attempt to save the struggling animal. It was rescued but the pack containing the instruments was lost. Cautley had to make the long journey to Edmonton to replace them.

The weather was glorious at the pass. For Wheeler it was exhilarating to be on the heights again, taking "good views", even if this meant starting up the mountain at five and returning at six in the evening. The snow mantled the peaks on September 1st; rain, wind, and hail battered their tents but they worked for another three weeks before Wheeler's men left for Assiniboine, occupying stations on the way.

From distant peaks Wheeler had seen Mount Assiniboine, its lofty summit towering 1,500 feet above its splendid entourage of mountains. With keen anticipation he approached it. The panorama which opened before him deepend his devotion to "The Great Hills". Against an autumn sky of deepest blue the magnificent triangular face, barred with horizontal bands of cliffs, rose like a mighty monolith above encircling lakes and glaciers where new-fallen snow glistened like an infinite profusion of jewels.

The nearby summit from which he saw it he christened "Wonder Peak".

Simpson Pass region, as photographed by A. O. Wheeler.

As Conrad Kain said: "Rightly did we christen it.... Far below... are two lakes fringed with pine and fir, blue-green and deep blue in their setting of white, Wonder and Marvel Lake." Another is Lake Gloria. Wheeler's nomenclature eloquently expresses his feelings. Camped in a larch grove, where the trees were ablaze with autumn colour, he undoubtedly shared Conrad's sentiments: "I think myself fortunate amidst the peace and quiet of nature."

He was in the field for five weeks after the Robson camp. When he returned to the Banff clubhouse it was an unexpected luxury to have Miss Savatard bring him "coffee and toast in bed".

The scenery between Banff and Assiniboine prompted an immediate visit to the Superintendent of Banff National Park with strong recommendations for clearing trails into the area. Since 1911 he'd been urging the Dominion government to assist in the construction of little log chalets at Moraine and O'Hara Lakes and in the Yoho Valley. "Such an arrangement... would bring in a totally different class of people... those who want to travel in the midst of Nature and study the great wonders of the Almighty without having to suffer a repletion of the effeteness of modern civilization from which they are striving to have a short reprieve." Within a few years the C.P.R. did build such chalets, which proved to be very popular and lucrative ventures.

But he felt that this should be "a paying industry for [the] Canadians" who would supply transport and guides. The developing situation was leaving the provision of pack trains and guides almost exclusively in the hands of "a monopoly" supported by the C.P.R. which "has driven most of the old and thoroughly competent [guides] from the district." Their work was taken over by "incompetent youths, who, decked in buckskins, swagger up and down the station platform and try to look like guides. Guides? God save the mark!" The Government should act "in no uncertain manner" to correct the situation, keeping in mind that it "holds this huge recreation ground in keeping on behalf of all the people of Canada...." Before the Robson expedition, his published address in Winnipeg strongly advocated access to some of the more remote regions of the Park and the "provision of accommodation for people of moderate means."

He and Conrad travelled by train to Crowsnest Pass in mid-October where he, Cautley, and Wallace agreed on monument sites. He closed the clubhouse, and late in October, after an absence of six months, he and Clara met in Victoria: "Put up at the Empress." An interesting letter from Oliver ("Lt. Oliver Wheeler, resident engineer, Meerut, India") brought news that he had passed his examinations in Hindustani and had enjoyed a hunting holiday in the Himalayan foothills. Riding an elephant had been a novel experience and "seeing the hills again was a treat." He wished, however, that he could have been at the Robson camp.

At the office in their Sidney home Wheeler resumed his winter survey work, writing reports, attending to business and Alpine Club correspondence, developing plates in the dark room, and superintending the long painstaking task of map-making, which was executed now by his extremely competent and skilful young draughtsman, Alan "Spike" Thomson. As Wheeler began his days at five in the morning and often worked evenings and Sundays, he expected his cartographer to do the same. One Sunday Thomson overheard Clara inquiring whether the young man really needed to put in such long hours. Her husband mumbled angrily, but she persisted with quiet firmness and Alan no longer had to work on Sundays. Wheeler's paternalism was combined with authoritarianism. But in sprightly old age, Alan "Spike" Thomson spoke with candour and affection about his chief: he felt that Wheeler's sense of purpose and high ideals had been good for him and had won for Wheeler the respect of his crews.

He and Clara took up their social life; continuing long-established habits. He frequently met ladies, including Miss Savatard, at the Empress for tea. On the 24th of May, Clara, Arthur, and her parents enjoyed a picnic with friends and they saw him off for Banff.

Miss Savatard met him as he walked up the road to the clubhouse where soon "all hands were busy" preparing for the survey. She accompanied him to Calgary again for Alpine Club supplies. His sister, Josephine, had lived in Calgary since 1912 where her husband, the Reverend George Jacob Bousfield, was assistant rector at the Pro-Cathedral—today's Church of the Holy Redeemer. He always visited her when in town and this time Miss Savatard went with him. The daughter of an Anglican priest, she was quite at home in the household. They all spent the evening at the "Orpheus Vaudeville". Back in Banff, he was delighted to find that she was soon "helping with the photos" in the map room.

Campbell and the men had been in the field since early June in the Crowsnest Pass, and on July 8th Wheeler and Conrad joined them and Cautley's

Thomson and companion cut up a mountain goat for Wheeler's favorite soup.

party for a week. Work in the Crowsnest system of passes occupied them for two seasons.

Arrangements had been made for the Club camp, and a group of Calgary members prepared the site in the Upper Yoho. Carrying packs, Wheeler and Conrad walked from Field to Takkakaw Falls and Wheeler was "pretty tired" when he arrived. He had returned to Camp in time for the annual meeting, but the carefree camaradarie which usually prevailed was missing. News had arrived of the outbreak of the First World War.

On August 12th he was back in the field, often putting in twelve-hour days. The topographical division worked at Crowsnest, Tent, Ptolemy, North Kootenay, Middle Kootenay, and Akamina passes. By mid-September the snows came, and moving camp, they got "bedding and selves soaked" where timber showered them with snow. But soon the tents were up and on days when weather prevented work, he was happy "making camp snug", mending clothes and boots, and listening to Conrad's enchanting tales of adventure.

Cautley's work was held up one day when two bears entertained themselves while the men watched in helpless frustration. The building of his boundary monuments involved digging three-foot holes for the cement foundations; the total amount of material for each monument averaged two thousand pounds which had to be packed five miles from the source of supply. The playful bruins kept the men at a safe distance while they tumbled bags of cement into the holes, scattered the gravel about, and dragged one bag a quarter of a mile into the bush.

When the season was drawing to a close, Wheeler moved camp through dense forest along a stream from Middle Kootenay Pass; the trail soon disappeared in a tangle of underbrush and they followed the bed of the stream ("must have crossed it a hundred times") in order to avoid the flanking cliffs. Cautley camped at one point in three feet of snow at Akamina Pass. Wheeler and Wallace joined them there but rain and snow halted operations and they "had some tough trailmaking in the snow" before they reached Pincher Creek station.

In Calgary he bought little gifts for Clara and Miss Savatard and once again breakfast in bed in the clubhouse was most acceptable. His rheumatism was relieved in Dr. Brett's hot pools and Miss Savatard went with him to Calgary where he attended Boundary Commissioners' meetings. She stayed at the Empress Hotel and he "put up at the Braemar", run by his long-standing friend, Miss Mollison, with whom he "chatted till midnight."

On the last day of October Clara met him in Victoria. As in many homes across the land, the shadow of war hung heavily. In mid-October Clara had written that Oliver's company was ready to be posted for duty; weeks later he and Clara got "a letter from Oliver. Place unknown." Their social life now involved patriotic activities: military dinners and balls, I.O.D.E. concerts and Red Cross work to raise money for war relief. All attention focussed on news of the War. Just before Christmas he helped Clara address invitations for a party, and soon their hospitable cottage overflowed with fifty-eight happy children whose fathers were overseas.

Oliver was one of the officers in charge of the Indian contingent fighting in France. Early in 1915 Arthur and Clara received a wire. With what anguish those communications were opened! Oliver had been "mentioned in dispatches." A few days later Wheeler wrote a letter of condolence to his old Calgary friend,

Dr. Bell-Irving—his son had been killed. When Wheeler had been in Calgary earlier, he had met "Mrs. Wooley-Dodd who told me Oliver had been killed." It was only a rumour but it gave him some extremely anxious moments. Thankfully, Clara wasn't exposed to that shock.

At Banff in early June he and Miss Savatard walked the trail to Sulphur Mountain Observatory. She was in need of consolation—her brother had been killed.

Field work began in June at Akamina Pass, one and a half miles north of the International Boundary. The trails were "rotten"; all the men had sore feet, and hordes of mosquitoes "drove them mad". But from the heights beautiful Cameron and Waterton Lakes sparkled with silvery ripples, and the eye traced the watershed from peak to peak. When they were marking the place where the watershed intersects the International Boundary they found "that it occurs on the flat summit of a little grassy col, with a few larch trees upon it, which makes a gap between the two steep ridges of rock. No more suitable spot could have happened for the International Boundary to cross the main range of the Rockies...." It was marked by a six-foot iron pillar visible for miles, both north and south. Along the great distance of the boundary between the two nations the only sentinels that guard the line are those silent monuments.

As Don Thomson rightly observes in *Men and Meridians:* "The heroic deeds of explorer-surveyors, [men] like Champlain, Mackenzie, Thompson and Fraser, are the stuff of legend and rightfully enjoy prominence in the story of Canada's development. But the work of pioneer land, railway and boundary surveyors which helped to transform a vast wilderness into ordered growth, has seldom stirred public imagination. Yet these men, too, subdued the unknown and replaced ignorance with knowledge. The lives of frontier scouts, of cowboys, soldiers and mounties have become invested with a glamour not bestowed upon surveyors.... The bold advances of the Wolseley expedition of 1870 and of the Canadian mounted police in their famous trek from Dufferin to Fort Macleod in 1874 have become part of Canadian folklore. Yet, whether in treacherous muskeg west of the Lake of the Woods or on the seemingly limitless plains in the vicinity of Red River, on hundreds of miles to the west of that waterway, men in uniform found that dauntless surveyors had been there before them. It was, in fact, at the Wood Mountain survey depot, 430 miles west of Red River, a provisioning point of the international boundary-marking project, that Commissioner Macleod and his weary mounties obtained essential supplies that enabled them to continue their journey to the foothills of the Rockies."

The isolated monolith erected by his predecessors four decades before must have stirred in Wheeler a sense of satisfaction. He was rendering a similar service for his country.

At Akamina Pass, Cautley's men encountered a grizzly displaying less respect for one of their own newly built monuments. "He sat up on the base of the monument and endeavoured to wrench the top off, failing which, he bit it and left deep tooth marks grooved on the metal covering. It is needless to state that all these operations were watched through a transit at a safe distance."

Wheeler journeyed to Club camp in Ptarmigan Valley; attendance was small, with many members overseas. It rained and Wheeler "got up some flags and cursed the weather." But "the patriotic evening went off splendidly—some magnificent addresses."

Cautley began the move to North Fork Pass over a dreadful trail west of the watershed. When the weary crew reached their destination they immediately began the preliminary survey and the hard work of cutting the lines. Wheeler arrived and promptly told Cautley that he was surveying the wrong pass! He had taken the wrong trail and was at Tornado Pass. It must have been particularly galling to find that Wheeler was right. He had Bridgland's 1913 map to prove it.

They agreed to complete the work there. The pass is dominated by 10,169-foot Tornado Mountain; its "gigantic rock buttresses...and cavernous chimneys [were] awe inspiring." The day after his arrival Wheeler made a stiff climb: "...had a devil of a time." As he had hurried off without an ice axe, he used a hand axe until he lost that in the snow. Cautley was worried and sent men to search for him before he returned at 9:30 in the evening.

On two subsequent ascents they had "narrow escapes". Arriving on Tornado's ridge, they worked quickly as dark seething clouds rolled swiftly toward them. With the work complete, they started down. The clouds unleashed terrifying flashes of lightning; "severe shocks were felt by members of the party." Sheets of hail battered them and mountain streams became wildly rushing torrents, sending rockfalls crashing on all sides. Covering their heads with rucksacks, they hugged the cold rock face. Wheeler reported: "I never saw a mountain break loose like that before and can readily understand how a party caught in a bad place in such a storm might be lost. Still mountains are mountains, and you must take them as you find them."

Working under such arduous conditions, Wheeler's rheumatism plagued him; it was a welcome comfort to have monotonous camp fare supplemented by "a small delicatessen" Miss Savatard sent to camp.

They surveyed South Kootenay, Middle Kootenay, and North Fork Passes before September brought snow at Elk Pass and they returned to Banff by way of the Kananaskis and Spray Rivers.

Wheeler's men were treated to "a good feed" and he again bought a small gift for Clara. Aching joints were soothed at Dr. Brett's and before departing for home, on Thanksgiving Day, Miss Savatard served "excellent kidney pie, Christmas pudding and a fine plum cake." Puffing his meerschaum, he sat out on the observation car enjoying the trip through his beloved Selkirks, and on his return to Sidney he and Clara had lovely days "loafing in the sun at Brentwood. Glorious!"

Three weeks later he spent a weekend at Cameron Lake with Miss Savatard and her married sister, May Monks, who ran a tiny chalet at that remote and lovely Vancouver Island spot. Mr. Monks met him "at Parksville with a speeder" and they spent pleasant evenings chatting round the fire with a handful of visitors. Returning to the railway he got drenched and when he got home he "went to bed with the grippe."

While he and Clara were decorating the house for Christmas they received word that Oliver had been awarded the Cross of the Legion of Honour, one of France's highest awards for distinguished service. In February he received the Military Cross. That Oliver should be distinguishing himself as a military man in a long Wheeler tradition must have been immensely gratifying to his father but it did little to lighten the constant burden of concern and anxiety. For Clara the strain must have been severe.

In 1916 field work was delayed by a late spring and exceptionally heavy snowfalls. Cautley's party left Morley for Kananaskis Pass June 5th; a five-day journey brought them to Kananaskis Lakes but the route to the pass was snow-blocked. Two days later, excessive heat sent meltwaters roaring into the rivers, and at the lower lake a pack horse tumbled from the trail. In trying to rescue it, Cautley's head packer lost his life. Jacob Koller had been with Cautley since 1913, and the fatality cast a pall of gloom on all the party.

Cautley finally reached the Pass on snowshoes July 14th. Wheeler's party also spent days shovelling snow over Mud Pass but arrived the day after the accident. Occupying a station, he agreed with Cautley that the high, steep, and narrow pass didn't justify the time and expense of erecting monuments. To delineate the watershed the topographical party returned in August to the "wildly picturesque area" of North and South Kananaskis Passes where the lovely lakes are dotted with timbered islands in a setting of rugged peaks.

Tracing the Divide to Elk Pass, Wheeler saw the "striking peaks... dominated by Mount Joffre", which he named for "distinguished generals who have rendered such names immortal through their splendid service to France in the great world war now in progress." Similarly, in the Palliser Pass area he named high mountains to honour the Royal family—another example of his strong feelings for Empire.

The Club camp was again a small one and he resumed field work at Spray, White Man, and Assiniboine Passes. In mid-September he was at Assiniboine. His topographical work in 1913 surveyed the watershed—which passes over the great massif—and now, after an examination by Cautley, they agreed to do a monument survey. The weather, which early in the season had been so dismal, was perfect. Wheeler found the scenery even more enchanting, in spite of the grizzlies.

Cautley's men were immobilized again for an hour one day while one of the great beasts, perfectly aware of their presence, steadily excavated gophers. Fortunately Cautley's man was mounted when one attacked him. Wheeler and a companion spotted its tracks in the snow, each footprint measuring ten and a half inches. They stood stock still, scarcely daring to breathe as he ambled slowly toward them. It seemed a terribly long time, but finally he changed course slightly. They "both took to the trees." They had no gun and prudently waited in their perch until they were certain the bruin wouldn't return.

The Assiniboine survey closed the season, and Wheeler walked back to Banff through valleys ablaze with a living mosaic of autumn colours. He carefully estimated mileage for inclusion in a detailed recommendation to the Park Superintendent—a proposal to provide facilities for "a walking tour" to Assin-boine.

Each year it became a bigger wrench to leave Banff and its mountains. The now-familiar respite of baths, visits with Miss Savatard to a few good friends, attending St. George's Church with her occasionally, a day or two in Calgary, and leisurely work with Mr. Mitchell over the clubhouse fire in the evenings were very relaxing. The splendid weather lingered on into October and they paddled up the Bow for an evening picnic and returned "home by moonlight—a glorious summer night."

The memorable weeks at Assiniboine and Banff were as exhilarating as wine. With a sudden flash of exhuberance he took a canoe below Bow Falls and for five days camped and ran his craft as far as Exshaw: "Glorious...great...wind

*Snowed under in August at South Kananaskis
Pass.*

blowing a gale..." At fifty-six he was recapturing the thrill of the young man whose prowess with the paddle had won him prizes on the Ottawa River thirty years before.

As snow fell softly on pine-covered slopes, they left for Victoria where he and Clara celebrated their annual reunion at the Empress. Clara's health had improved and she went into Victoria several days a week; they attended church with her parents and spent "Christmas at Brentwood, games and dancing."

Wheeler's relationship with Miss Savatard was beginning to arouse "ribald comment" in Banff and among younger members of the Alpine Club. In her old age, his sister, Josephine (to whom he had introduced Miss Savatard in 1914) vehemently denied the gossip that "he'd been carrying on" an affair. If any of these comments had reached Wheeler's ear he would have ignored them with aristocratic disdain. His deep devotion to Clara is obvious, but sadly, she was incapable of continuing to share his zest for the rugged outdoor life. At thirty-six Miss Savatard was a robust, competent young woman who responded warmly to his friendship and revelled in camp life.

Wheeler was not insensitive in family relationships. He had many short-comings. Hypocrisy was not one of them.

On December 30th he took Miss Savatard home to meet Clara. The three of them had dinner in town and saw *Puss in Boots* at the Victoria Royal Theatre; Clara and Miss Savatard spent the night at Clara's club, and he stayed at his but joined them for breakfast. On New Year's Eve, after church service they sat up and "saw the New Year in". Friends called on New Year's Day and the house was gay. Next day Clara was "sick in bed. Stomach and heart."

Chapter XV

Wheeler was writing the first of the three-volume report on the Inter-provincial Boundary survey. Each chapter was sent to Cautley for editing and the book was finished in June along with the accompanying atlas. These books contain not only reports of each season's work but excellent photographs and detailed descriptions of the terrain and a brief history of each Pass. In four seasons the boundary had been surveyed, monumented, and mapped from Kicking Horse Pass south to the International Boundary.

In mid-May he and Miss Savatard left for Banff. Clara was with them. The day after their arrival the three of them "went for a stroll" and Clara was taken ill. Dr. Brett was summoned but after four days she "was walking abo_. a bit." In a hired car he took her sightseeing round the village; they had their photograph taken together, and she did the annual ordering of supplies in Calgary with him. After six weeks she returned to Sidney.

The Boundary Commissioners had agreed that the monument survey of Yellowhead Pass was urgent but there would be time to work at Howse Pass and make a preliminary assessment of what would be entailed on the survey from that point to Jasper. The necessary surveys for mapping the watershed from the summit of Bow Pass to historic Howse Pass were available from Wheeler's topographical work of 1903-1906.

The crews set out from Field and travelled to Howse Pass on the Emerald Lake road, then followed the trail to the high summit of Amiskwi Pass and made the sharp 2,500-foot descent to a tributary of the Blaeberry River. Cautley's contingent, who had made this journey a week earlier, spent two days cutting and shovelling snow to reach the Amiskwi trail summit. Wheeler found the route "most troublesome". One of the men in charge of the pack-train cut his thigh with an axe. Wheeler saved his life by staunching the serious hemmorrhage with the cook's bread dough.

They worked at Howse Pass for a month, but Wheeler left after two weeks for the Club camp. His team was instructed to occupy camera stations southward to Bow summit and erect the necessary monuments to mark the watershed which follows the crest of peaks rising boldly above the west side of the Mistaya River. When this work was finished they were to follow Cautley to Jasper along the Saskatchewan, Sunwapta, and Athabasca Rivers.

After Camp, Wheeler went by train, stopping in Edmonton to order and forward supplies to Jasper. James and William Macoun were studying and collecting the flora and fauna in Jasper Park, and Wheeler spent the weekend at Cavell Creek in James's camp and with William and his wife, who were camped on the Miette River. Campbell and Thomson, the advance guard of his party, met him there. "The boys had a jolly good supper ready for me."

He was not always so welcome back in camp. Morrison Bridgland, who worked with him for years, frankly confessed that he *hated* to see the return of the chief.

In Jasper Wheeler had picked up letters from Clara and a little package of delicacies from Miss Savatard. Thinking of the exciting journey awaiting him at the end of the season, he wrote and then wired her to join his party at Jasper. She refused.

Work at the Yellowhead was completed in a month and, with keen anticipation, Wheeler started on the route he'd heard about for years from his Alpine Club friends. He rode toward majestic, snowy Mount Edith Cavell. At the junction of the Whirlpool and the Athabasca they camped where autumn's gold and russet glowed against the dark spruce and in the blue haze; to the west rugged peaks flanked the Whirlpool valley. Here the Colemans had searched for the long-obliterated footsteps of fur-traders to David Thompson's famous Athabasca Pass.

Still proceeding south along the Athabasca, Wheeler's horses struggled over deadfall and on the fourth day they camped within site of snow-capped peaks marking a pass where the engaging young Walter Wilcox had crossed, searching for the legendary mountains at Athabasca pass in 1896. Next day the pack-train clambered up the steep northern approach of Wilcox Pass. Wheeler climbed to a camera station; across the deep valley of the Sunwapta he saw the great western escarpment where the vast Columbia Icefield spills over in awesome rivers of ice. There, English alpine friends, Collie, Stutfield, and Woolley had vainly tried to reach the crowning white cone of Mount Columbia.

Making the precipitous descent to the valley of the Saskatchewan, Wheeler could see where Mary Schäffer-Warren had turned up the valley which ended her long search for Maligne Lake. With her friend Mary Adams and guides Fred Warren and Sidney Unwin, they were the first party to record a southern approach to the famous lake. When she married Fred Warren in 1915 Mary made her home in Banff and remained one of Clara and Arthur's closest friends.

At the end of the ten-day trip Wheeler was only too anxious to probe the beckoning valleys and climb the outlying spurs he had seen. Next season's surveys looked promising indeed.

Before leaving Banff for Victoria he bought the plot he and Clara had chosen in the little pine-encircled cemetery.

In February he came as invited guest-official to the Banff Winter Carnival. Starting in a very modest way, the villagers had "managed to put Banff on the map" as a winter resort. School children spent days building ice statues to line the streets; an illuminated ice palace was erected where the Carnival Queen was crowned, and the little village celebrated exuberantly.

Miss Savatard had remained in Banff and had an advertisement placed in the local paper offering "private cookery lessons for adults and children."

Even with the influx of winter visitors for the Carnival it is unlikely that there would have been enough response to earn a living and she probably had paying guests in her large rented cottage. Wheeler "settled in [there] and spent the evening chatting." The next few days were a whirlwind of activity. With Miss Savatard he went to the curling matches, swim races, hockey games, and figure skating exhibitions on the Bow, and acted as judge at the ski jump.

It was Conrad Kain who had introduced the local boys to this sport. Naturally he believed that every boy should know how to make his own skis and master that alpine delight. Soon the young men he had coached would develop Banff as a major ski resort. In the evening Wheeler was judge at the toboggan slide which was "as slick as grease", and brightly festooned with Japanese lanterns. Bundled in warm clothing, bright toques and sashes, gay groups of young and old careened down the slopes, and puffed and panted back up to warm themselves round the blazing bonfire and enjoy hot dogs and steaming coffee served in the refreshment tent. The culminating event was the great "Ball in Brewster's Opera House", which was decorated with bunting and coloured lights. The ladies' gowns were opulent: "...pale green satin with silver over-dress...blue velvet *en train* with oriental trim...black moire taffeta and cream silk..."; young girls were demure in gowns of white embroidered organdy.

On Wheeler's return to Sidney, he wrote enthusiastically to the Commissioner of National Parks about the potential of this winter festival, undoubtedly adding a few suggestions for improvements!

Clara came with him to Banff in early May where Miss Savatard welcomed them at the clubhouse. On their thirtieth wedding anniversary, Clara, Arthur—and Miss Savatard—were "motored out to the Loop for a picnic, perfect day; very enjoyable outing."

On July 1st, he and Clara took the train to Field where he was ready to set out for the Howse Pass survey. After a short walk he took her back to the hotel in the evening and said good-bye. He then joined Thomson at the nearby camp, ready for an early morning start. On impulse he walked all the way back next morning to have breakfast with her, and to bid her a touching second farewell.

Wheeler was a man of action, and his busy life left little time for probing his emotions. But in this incident there is a suggestion that his conscience was troubling him. His feelings toward Miss Savatard were deepening and his beloved Clara's health was failing. Was her condition being worsened by awareness of the situation?

He went on to his work at the Freshfield Glacier, where he crossed a three-mile snowfield, negotiated a thousand-foot rock climb, and fell into a gaping crevasse. After a few anxious moments, his men rescued him. His back was hurt but in his diary he records: "Felt pretty good after three such hard days."

In order to examine the British Columbia side of Bush Pass he and his men had to pack a camp outfit on their backs, as the Pass was impossible for loaded horses. One packer left and Wheeler returned to Banff to hire a replacement and to attend the small Club camps in Paradise and Consolation valleys.

In his absence Campbell ably continued the work, climbing "Coronation Mountain". During the war years it was difficult to hire good men and the two

*Clara Wheeler and Miss Savatard enjoying a
picnic.*

accompanying Campbell were novices. On the descent, he had to lower them over a cliff with a rope. The instruments and a rucksack containing the field notes were lowered, and one of the men untied the packages and placed the rucksack on a narrow ledge. It immediately bounded off into space! For two days, in pouring rain, they searched for the vital notebooks in vain. The stations had to be re-occupied. Wheeler's report states that this happened on "Campbell Glacier." His assistant certainly deserved the honor of having his name bestowed on *that* glacier.

When he returned, camp was pitched on the gravel flats of the Saskatchewan east of Howse Pass. Here the great fur-trader-surveyor-explorer, David Thompson, had waited for the snow to melt in 1807, and that spring he had set out to search for a pass leading to the legendary Columbia River. He was successful, but ironically, the pass wasn't named for him. Wheeler christened a fine mountain flanking it "Mount David".

Wheeler toiled for five hours to a camera station on its ridge and the clouds descended like a shroud. He waited for hours before coming down. His party was greatly relieved when they finally saw him approaching: "Boys had caught three little trout and had them ready for my supper." In a few days he walked ahead to scout for trail and campsites at Glacier Lake where "fine stations" were occupied on "very satisfactory days".

He saw "the towering heights of Mount Forbes, the highest and most striking peak of this portion of the main range..." It was named in 1858 by the energetic and able young Dr. Hector, member of the Palliser expedition. The intrepid Hector and his Metis guide, Erasmus, had done some dangerous climbing in the area—in their bare feet! Wheeler fell while crossing a glacier and once more his back bothered him "quite a bit", but he "enjoyed the station nonetheless."

Moving camp north along the Saskatchewan (the route of today's scenic highway) to its junction with the Alexandra, they camped on the broad shingle flats. In the evening Wheeler sat outside by the fire and wrote up his field notes, diary, and correspondence. The solitude was broken only by the soothing sound of horses cropping grass, the jingle of their bells, and the ripple of water over gravel. In the northwest the sun disappeared behind the uplifted horizon; the sky of palest turquoise shaded into aqua and merged with glowing apricot—a backdrop for the black bastion of Mount Saskatchewan with its weird pinnacles, needles, and towers. The meandering river flowed from the mountain in ribbons of silver. On the way to Thompson Pass they "slept in the open...glorious blaze of stars. The Great Hills all around."

The watershed had been traced to the towering guardians of the Lyell and Freshfield icefields. Making the stiff climb to the summit of Thompson Pass, they occupied seven stations during twelve days in the area. The Pass was named for the American climber, C. S. Thompson, who crossed it in 1900. Finding this route had made it possible for the Reverend James Outram to make the first ascent of Mount Columbia in 1902, thus depriving Professor Collie of the peak he had tried so hard to reach ever since he, Stutfield, and Woolley had first looked out upon the massive extent of the Icefield in 1897.

Collie had attempted to reach the peak in 1900 by way of the narrow, heavily timbered Bush Valley on the west. His party's bushwacking was "full of woe", as Wheeler noted. His own travel in the valley during 1918 and 1919 was equally so. On their last attempt to descend in order to get topographical information, the pack horses rolled down the slopes and one animal was so badly hurt it had to be shot.

Wheeler was an excellent horseman, but he often had sharp disagreements with the man in charge of the pack-trains. To these men the horses were an investment and from long experience they knew what the animals could do. Wheeler, always impatient and anxious to get on with the job, didn't worry unduly about expecting them to undertake what the packers knew was impossible. This was certainly the case in the Bush valley incident. They were very fortunate to lose only one horse. Work would have been delayed if more had been killed.

From the stations climbed round Thompson Pass, Wheeler looked out onto the Columbia Icefield, a glistening sea of ice and snow, bounded only by the peaks on the horizon: the white cone of Columbia, the dark forbidding precipices of Mount Alberta and the North Twin, the Snow Dome and Mount Stutfield, "the giant upholding buttresses of the icefield." The icefields which straddle the watershed with their great burden of ice, give birth to rivers flowing thousands of miles to empty into the Pacific, the Arctic, and the Atlantic Oceans.

With keen anticipation Wheeler contemplated the challenging work the area would provide next season. It was now late autumn and they retraced their route to the Saskatchewan River; food was dangerously low and they hurried on to Lake Louise station. It had been a strenuous three months. His side and back were painful and he felt "poorly and run down" so he recuperated for a month in Banff. By Thanksgiving Day he felt fit enough for "a tramp to the Hoodoos" in the Bow valley for a picnic with Miss Savatard.

He had a throbbing infected thumb when he and Clara met at the Empress in November and was home in bed with a fever until the eleventh. Clara served him breakfast in bed. When they received the electrifying news that the Armistice had been signed, his illness was forgotten. He immediately "hoisted the Union Jack" and went into Victoria with Clara where they picked up Clara's sister, Nellie Everall, her husband and daughter and "did the town".

Clara and Arthur were amongst those who had cause for rejoicing. Their son was safe. All across the land people thronged the streets to celebrate. In Victoria "the town went wild"—downtown, automobile horns blared, cyclists and street cars added to the din, and jostling crowds cheered themselves hoarse until far into the night.

The feelings of a man with Wheeler's background expressed those felt by many at the time. In ringing phrases, he immediately wrote his Director's greeting to Club members: "The War is over! The arms of the Allies are crowned with Glorious victory! Our Empire is safe! Right has triumphed over might! Thank God!"

Early in the new year Miss Savatard rented a cottage in Victoria. She carefully considered the move and the proposal that she might help in Wheeler's office in Sidney part-time. She went with Clara and Arthur to the Vancouver Island Alpine Club banquet and all three were frequently house guests of the Everalls; she and her sister came for dinner, and in mid-January, she was working in the office. In June the office was moved to Banff, and he and Miss Savatard had their annual May picnic on the Bow.

When the survey crew assembled at Thompson Pass again, Conrad was with them. In 1917 he had married the housekeeper of his good friends, the American climbers, Mr. and Mrs. A. H. MacCarthy, and settled down to a quiet life of farming and trapping at Wilmer in the Windermere Valley. He was determined to cut all ties with the Alpine Club lest he be tempted to go climbing again. But the lure was too strong when he heard that Wheeler was going to the Columbia Icefields. He applied for work and Wheeler was delighted to have him back.

The futile attempt to reach Bush River delayed them for weeks, but on July 19th they were camped on a beautiful site where the Saskatchewan flows from the Columbia Icefield. On the west side of the depression rise awesome cliff walls; the mile-wide river of ice creeps to its fissured gravel bed, flanked on the east by a high park-like ridge dotted with alplands and clumps of evergreen.

Conrad led a climbing party to the Icefield and started the long trek toward Mount Columbia. He was exhilarated. This was virgin alpine terrain for him. As on the first excursion to Robson, however, the crowning summit of Columbia was not to be his. All about him were great peaks—eight over eleven thousand feet. However, by the end of the season's survey he had led the way to high camera stations, including those on outlying crests of Mount Columbia and the shoulders of awesome Mount Alberta, Mount Athabasca, and Mount Saskatchewan. (In 1923 he returned with an American party to lead the second ascent of Mount Columbia and other splendid climbs among these monarchs of the Icefield.)

With work in the capable hands of his assistants, Wheeler left for the "Victory Camp" of the Club, held on the shore of Yoho Lake. He found "camp well constructed and quite lively." In his Director's address round the fire he referred with pride to the 113 Alpine Club members who had served in the War and reverently of "those eleven who will never again answer the roll call amidst the Great Hills.... They have made the traditions of the Alpine Club glorious forever!" He outlined plans for the "Homecoming Camp" to be held at Assiniboine the next year and forcefully announced that he intended to "place my resignation in the hands of the executive members so that all will have an opportunity to express their approval or disapproval" of his war-time policy.

Apparently there had been murmurs of dissatisfaction about holding camps during the war. He acknowledged that this may have been a mistake. Perhaps it had been an unsound policy financially, with so few members attending during those years. His directing activities at camp gave him such immense satisfaction that he had probably never considered discontinuing the camps. But he was fifty-nine years old; the lads who had left for War would return as mature young men with new ideas about running the Club.

Already others were taking over part of his role and he spent the time quietly, but happily in camp. In mid-week he walked to Emerald Lake to meet Clara. He saddled a pony and "led her into camp. She stood the journey well and felt quite comfortable." The ride included fording the swirling Yoho River. She received an enthusiastic welcome after an absence of so many years but collapsed next day. His diary records: "Had a fair night but heart not very good." Doggedly she had come to the clubhouse in early July. Now she rallied and returned there after a few days where she "had supper ready" when he, Miss Savatard, and others returned from the side trip to measure the Yoho Glacier.

On August 12th Wheeler was back with the survey at Wilcox Pass where he took up his camera work; the climb to the station on the shoulder of Mount Alberta left him exhausted. They descended into the valley of the Sunwapta,

The raft "Fortress Queen" used for a season's work at Fortress Lake.

where work was hampered by constant cloud and rain, and ascended the west branch of the Athabasca. At its head rose Mount Columbia. He and Conrad were enchanted with the view of the mountain from this vantage point. Mary Schäffer's party had been up this valley in 1907. They too had gazed with wonder at the graceful glacier-draped pyramid rising sharply from the low valley: "a beautiful example of exquisite symmetry." Altogether ten camera stations were used to map the Icefield area and delineate the erratic course of the watershed there.

They then cut trail to Fortress Lake where Conrad and all hands constructed a raft which they grandly christened "Fortress Queen"; it held five and Conrad distinguished himself in navigating it with oars and sail. Camera and monument work occupied eleven days and on September second they started back for the essential climb of Sunwapta Peak; persistently bad weather had foiled their earlier attempts. Wheeler and Campbell started at daylight on a fine morning. Hours later the snow came; they pushed on to the summit but the weather didn't improve. They were in a "much colder and exposed position now." At the last minute the clouds broke, and working feverishly for two hours, they accomplished their task. The clouds immediately closed in and they had to grope their way back down the mountain.

On October 1st he was back in Banff and five days later, he, Ralph Rink, and Miss Savatard started for Assiniboine. They were snowbound and he "helped her make meals and cleared the snow to make her tent snug." He and Ralph played checkers and discussed plans for forming a business partnership.

His advocacy of trails to Assiniboine hadn't resulted in any action by Park officials so he decided to inaugurate the "Assiniboine Walking and Riding Tours" himself. He was also writing to his good friend, Col. Longstaff, about an important Alpine Congress. And to Parks Commissioner Harkin about a "plot of land I want near Middle Springs."

Chapter XVI

"I want" are the operative words. He had made up his mind to live as much as possible—and to die, in Banff.

And Clara? Her place was at his side. She had a deep conviction about that. Like her Quaker ancestors she was capable of tenderness and consideration for those she loved. But she had an independent will (and quiet pride) equal to that of her husband and that of the younger woman whose presence threatened a warm relationship that had endured long separations for over three decades.

When Arthur went to the Winter Carnival in Banff in February Clara was with him. They had rented a house for the month and she went to the events, including the ball where they stayed until one a.m.

He spent most of his time planning the Assiniboine Tours. Appealing to the Commissioner of Dominion National Parks, he got some financial support from the federal and British Columbia governments; the Banff Park Superintendent, J. M. Wardle, co-operated by selling blankets, tents, and war surplus supplies. Costs had to be kept to a minimum to achieve his aim of keeping fees within reach of those who couldn't afford guides, packers, horses, and equipment: all-inclusive charges were only five dollars a day. He and Ralph Rink invested $2,500 and Clara $500; Miss Savatard also invested, and at some point the Alpine Club participated in the business. He designed and sent out illustrated circulars, placing thousands of them in the C.P.R. hotels and chalets as well as in local hotels.

It was a 75-mile round trip with permanent camps strategically situated amidst superb scenery. Completely equipped tents (and eventually small log huts at some points) were planned for Eau Claire on the Spray River, Trail Centre, near Spray Lakes, Wonder Lodge, Golden Valley, Sunshine Valley, and Assiniboine. The tours would leave Banff from the main camp at Middle Springs twice weekly during July, August, and September. Ralph Rink was in charge of the pack-train and ladies with the help of cooks acted as managers and hostesses at each camp. Before July the trails would have to be cut out, camps erected, supplied, and manned, but with preliminary work completed, he and Clara went home where a wire awaited them. "Oliver will start for home April 12th".

As well as the usual survey reports and *Canadian Alpine Club Journal* editing, he now had to put finishing touches to a project he had started in October. When he had learned that "a Congress of Alpinism was to be held in Monaco in May, 1920 under the patronage of His Royal Highness le Prince de Monaco and the Presidency of M. le Baron Gabet, President du Club Alpin Français to embrace the great Alpine Clubs...of the Allied Nations", he "proceeded forthwith to prepare a suitable representation that would place before the Congress the outstanding features and magnificent scenic attractions of the Canadian Rockies and the high mountain ranges of the Yukon."

Volleys of correspondence were fired in all directions. Commissioner Harkin agreed to pay the expense of sending a delegate; Tom Longstaff got a letter and used his influence to ensure good coverage for the Canadian exhibition. Professional colleagues H. F. J. Lambart of the Geodetic Survey, contributed to a paper on glaciers in the Yukon; Morrison Bridgland and Campbell supplemented Wheeler's own paper on the application of photography to the mapping of the Rockies—his presentation also included a report on glaciology; geologist E. M. Burwash agreed to do a paper, and N. B. Sanson of Banff wrote on Climatology. Photographer Byron Harmon was the official delegate; he and Wheeler selected "a magnificent exhibit of photographic enlargements and unsurpassed motion films...." Included were some of Wheeler's photos from high stations and some exquisitely hand-painted photographs of mountain flora by Mrs. Schäffer-Warren and Julia Henshaw.

The exhibit was a resounding success, with Harmon's films bringing standing ovations. Wheeler had scored again on behalf of the Alpine Club of Canada. Characteristically, all the material "was duly presented as a gift to the Club Alpin Français at the close of the Congress." And Wheeler cabled Baron de Gabet that he had been elected an Honourary member of the Alpine Club of Canada.

The Prince of Monaco recognized Wheeler's contribution by naming him an Officer of the Order of St. Charles and conferring upon him the Cross of the Order; the Italian Alpine Club subsequently presented him with a splendid alpine cape and hat. He wore it with immense pride and flair.

How gratifying it would have been for Wheeler to be present. But business and professional duties were extremely demanding that year, and furthermore, he would have missed Oliver's homecoming.

In the midst of a tremendously busy schedule, he dashed to Victoria on May 23rd bringing Clara a gift to celebrate the occasion. Next day they hired a car and driver and with the Everalls hurried to the wharf. "Soon found Oliver in uniform." they had not seen their son for eight years.

Always outwardly composed, the reunion was profoundly moving for Clara. They had lunch at Everalls and dinner at home; next day Oliver was proudly introduced to his father's colleagues and the Surveyor General and in the evening, "had a swell dinner—turkey and lots of refreshments."

The Sidney house was gay for weeks. At thirty, Oliver, with neatly-trimmed moustache, dark flashing eyes, and the "aristocratic" Wheeler nose, was very handsome in his Major's uniform. He had his mother's unassuming manner (in later years friends said "he was modest in the extreme"), but more than one Charleston-dancing, bobbed-hair flapper was attracted by the Wheeler charm as he plucked out the jazz tunes of the day and whistled a syncopated accompaniment.

After two days his father had to return to Banff where he and Miss Savatard had been working since April. They had celebrated his sixtieth birthday weekend with a special dinner ("Miss Savatard made me a fine plum cake") and their picnic on the Bow.

A letter had arrived from relatives in California about his brother Willie: "Jolly row on!" It seemed that the fifty-year-old Willie was either separated from his second wife or forming a new liaison. Without warning he arrived in Banff on the night train a few days later.

Neither of the brothers had changed very much in intervening years. Arthur still thought some good hard work would cure what ailed him, and in short order Willie was "at chores", replenishing the wood pile and taking down shutters. After two days: "...did chores myself. Willie indisposed...leaves clubhouse. Gone I don't know where. Paid him $12 for work and expenses."

Heavy snows and a very late spring seriously hampered the Walking Tour, the Club camp, and the survey. Campbell and his men had to travel to Jasper by train in mid-June and the packhorses which were to take them to Fortress Lake didn't arrive for another week. Wheeler dashed out by train to get supplies and horses and saw Oliver off with Campbell up the Athabasca. Oliver hadn't seen the Jasper country and was delighted to be occupying stations with the men for several weeks—when climbing in the Rockies, he was using his "muscles of happiness".

He had been commissioned by the British government to determine the suitability of Canadian methods of photo-topographical surveying for use in the high mountains of India. Wheeler's crew were very pleased to have him in the field—his warm manner was free of the condescension his father sometimes displayed.

It was fortunate that Campbell and Thomson were so well trained that work could be left in their hands as, except for one day, Wheeler didn't get to the field until late in August. And he was equally lucky that Oliver was on hand in Banff that summer.

Clara had arrived at the clubhouse in June, and immediately she and "all hands" under Wheeler's directions began working furiously to get the Walking Tour in shape. Miss Savatard and three other young women were sent to camp, while axemen were still cutting trails. Clara was in charge at the clubhouse and was helping to sort out the tons of equipment. Oliver took over supervision of some construction workers and by the time Club camp opened, matters were almost in hand, although there was some confusion—most unusual in Wheeler's well-run camps.

"The Homecoming Camp" he had so carefully planned was a success even though he had worn himself out preparing for it. It could only be held at magnificent Mount Assiniboine because the Walking Tour trails were ready; all previous camps had been near the railway to facilitate transportation. Camp opening was delayed for weeks, however, because snow often halted trail-making. But old friends Mumm and Inderbinen were there to welcome the heroes of battle, and at the annual meeting there was an "expression of gratitude to the Director for carrying the Club through the war and making Assiniboine camp in the face of extraordinary difficulties." His resignation was not accepted.

With Clara at the clubhouse and the camp at Middle Springs, and Oliver on hand to keep an eye on the Tours, Wheeler finally left for the field. The day

Oliver Wheeler with his parents.

he arrived in Jasper, Oliver wired him about forest fires in the Simpson River valley. He had to hurry back; he had patrons and expensive equipment on those trails. It was a relief to find that fire fighters and wardens had it under control when he made his inspection.

On August 23rd he and Clara said good-bye to Oliver. He was off to Toronto and England on his way to join the Survey of India.

Clara was withstanding remarkably well a year of physical and emotional stress. On January 8th her eldest brother had died at the early age of fifty-eight. For the Professor this was a profound loss. Jim had worked so closely with him and carried on his work with distinction, ranging as far as the Bering Sea; at the time of his death he was head of the Biological Division of the Geological Survey of Canada.

His father had been remarkably well and active, happily absorbed the last few years in writing his memoirs. But the death of his son robbed life of its zest. Six months later, almost to the day, he died.

Clara had to travel to the funeral alone. Only the pressure of work could have kept Arthur from attending, for he was very devoted to the Professor. During the previous winter he had spent nearly every evening reading to him and helping him with his manuscript. It was published posthumously and clearly reveals the sheer joy and satisfaction with which the old botanist looked back over the years. His child-like naiveté and candid expression of pride in his achievements are delightful.

The satisfaction was justifiable. He was one of Canada's most able, colourful, enthusiastic, and far-ranging pioneer scientists.

Two days after Oliver's departure, Wheeler was at last in the field in the Whirlpool Valley, ascending to famed Athabasca Pass. "The boys put up my tent and made me comfortable."

They had worked wonderfully well. Considerable time had been spent at Fortress Lake and while Oliver was with them they had climbed in view of twelve-thousand-foot Mount Clemenceau and examined its extenstive glaciers and icefields. Twelve dozen plates had been exposed when Wheeler joined them. Soon he was climbing and happily spending many a "beautiful evening in such a lovely place." September snows halted work and the same conditions prevailed as they moved on to Canoe and Fraser Pass. By September 28th they knew they would have to return next year to finish the work.

Wheeler closed up the Assiniboine camps, and he and Miss Savatard had their Thanksgiving outing. In mid-October he went by train to Rogers Pass looking for a possible site for next year's camp. Carrying a heavy pack, he walked twelve miles in the snow to one of his old Selkirk camps at Bear Creek where he made "a snug camp in the bush". Campsites weren't suitable but for three days, in solitude, he "enjoyed walk along track — and old scenes and associations." In mid-November at Banff, he said good-bye to Miss Savatard who was going to visit relatives in England.

One of the first things he did on his return to Sidney was to walk with Clara "across the field to visit the Professor's grave."

When he, Clara, and Nellie's young daughter, Eleanor, "saw the New Year in" they had something special to celebrate.

Oliver had kept in touch with the Longstaffs and the Wedgewoods (with whom he had spent such enjoyable weeks on the 1910 excursions) while he was stationed in England with the Royal Engineers. When Mrs. Wedgewood heard

A. J. Campbell and Alan S. Thomson in a crevasse on Mount Chaba's glacier.

he was stopping over on his way to India she invited him to spend a weekend at her country home. She wanted to have congenial young companions for him and was disappointed to find that they were nearly all away.

Fortunately, a good friend was available: a lovely, fine young sportswoman, Miss Dorothea (Dolly) Danielsen. When Oliver left the Wedgewoods he was engaged! He left immediately for India; she followed in a few months, as the wedding had been arranged for March. The year 1921 was a memorable one for Oliver.

His father, meanwhile, organized the Assiniboine Tours much more satisfactorily. Headquarters were on the plot he had leased at Middle Springs on a bench of Sulphur Mountain with a superb view overlooking the town and valley. There the tents were pitched at the edge of the clearing; the scent of, pine and fir filled the air; on the mossy forest floor delicate calypso orchids grew in drifts of rose and brilliant lilies flashed their orange banners in the green grass.

Here Clara came to work early in June, unpacking mounds of camping equipment: seventy mattresses, linen, lounge chairs, dining utensils; she shopped with Arthur for supplies in Calgary and for three months supervised the cook and acted as hostess in the large dining marquee. Guests not wishing to make the tour could just relax in her pleasant camp. Riders and hikers could take in as much of the six-day tour as they wished and, as one visitor remarked, "the meals are 'super'; blankets, mattresses and most cordial attentions to our every comfort await us at each camp."

On June 9th the survey in Campbell's charge left to complete work at Fortress Lake and on June 27th Wheeler and Cautley were placing the monuments there. Following the Athabasca, he and Campbell worked toward Athabasca Falls where Wheeler left the party to return to Banff. Campbell and Thomson occupied the stations necessary to cover the distance between the Falls and the Whirlpool River. They were then to proceed up the Whirlpool.

At Middle Springs Arthur found Clara "had everything quite nice but it's pretty soggy"; later in the season he slept in her tent one night and found that it leaked.

He dashed off to Assiniboine on an inspection trip. Miss Savatard had her camp in good order and at Eau Claire he spent time with "a very happy lot" and saw them on their way. Two of the party were Dr. Winthrop Stone, President of Purdue University, and his wife, who had spent so many happy summers climbing the high trails in the Rockies. They were on their way to Mount Eon, a challenging peak in the Assiniboine group.

One reason Wheeler derived such satisfaction from combining his surveys with the Walking Tours was that he was able to provide information, maps and access to some of the great unclimbed mountains in the vicinity. "To feel a passing pleasure in a general view of the mountains from afar is worthwhile; but to tramp through the forest, scramble over the moraine, work a course across glaciers, traverse ice slopes and then grapple with the cliffs, couloirs and chimneys until the summit is gained — that stimulates one's respect and reverence for them...."

Back at Athabasca Pass on July 19th, he climbed on Mount Brown and twice on Punchbowl Ridge, placing monuments: "good climb — not very tired." With his sense of history he was delighted to make an examination of this celebrated pass.

Miss Savatard, left, with cook at Wonder Lodge on the Assiniboine Walking Tour.

The old trail of the fur traders was gone, and legendary Mount Brown and Mount Hooker had been dethroned from the place of eminence they had occupied on maps since 1829. But Mount Hooker and its icefield were as impressive as they had been when the botanist, David Douglas, initiated the legend; he had named the mountain for the same Dr. Hooker whom Professor Macoun had consulted about botanical specimens early in his career.

The little tarn which straddles the summit of Athabasca Pass, sending its waters to the Arctic and the Pacific, was still as peaceful as it had been when Sir George Simpson, the Little Emperor of the Hudson's Bay Company, named it "The Committee's Punch Bowl". Sir George, among his other outstanding attributes, had a keen eye for what might enhance his career and had astutely named it in honour of his superiors, the Governing Committee of the Company.

Near the summit Cautley's men found a few corroded musket balls that David Thompson had left behind 109 years before. He and his Indian guide had found this pass in 1811 when the Peigan Indians had turned him back from Howse Pass which he had used to transport furs from the Pacific via the Columbia River.

Wheeler and his men moved on to nearby Whirlpool Pass and on July 25th he left to attend Club camp at O'Hara meadows.

Park Superintendent Stronach met him with the tragic news that Dr. Stone had been killed on Mount Eon. "He turned the matter of the accident over to me."

Dr. Stone and his wife were experienced climbers. They had been within a few feet of the summit when he unroped to examine a difficult spot above. With ghastly suddenness Mrs. Stone saw him hurtle over her head. The slab of rock on which he sought a handhold had broken off and carried him to his death below. She carefully inched her way down until she was trapped on a narrow ledge. Wearing only knickers and flannel shirt, she awaited rescue for eight days—without food. Famous packer-guide Bill Peyto of Banff, Swiss guide Rudolph Aemmer, and an R.C.M.P. officer found her. Aemmer carried her down. Club member Dr. Fred Bell hurried from Assiniboine camp to administer medical attention and a stretcher party started, taking her by easy stages toward Banff. Wheeler rushed to meet them and "took Dr. Bell's place at the stretcher". At Trail Centre she rested and Wheeler returned to Banff to meet her son whom he had wired.

A strong climbing party was mustered for the dangerous task of recovering Dr. Stone's body. The MacCarthys and Conrad Kain, Aemmer, and Edouard Feuz succeeded in the gallant effort. Wheeler and Clara made arrangements at the funeral chapel and the hospital and consoled the bereaved wife and son. In the interval Wheeler spent one day at the Assiniboine camp. When he had seen the Stones safely off on the train he was exhausted from physical and emotional strain. He was always keenly concerned about the safety of any climbing parties and the shock of the tragedy was deeply felt.

On the day the Stones departed, Sir Otway Wheeler-Cuffe, Third Baronet, and Lady Wheeler-Cuffe arrived on the night train. Arthur and Clara called on them at the Mount Royal Hotel and his second cousin and his wife gladly accepted the invitation to stay at Middle Springs. Sir Otway was taken on an overnight trip to Eau Clair camp and Clara had a tea for them before they left three days later. Although Arthur kept in touch with them he never saw them again.

Sir Otway had succeeded to the Baronetcy in 1915 but hadn't returned to his county position in Kilkenny until his retirement from a distinguished career in India; he was now on his way home to Lyrath House. He was the last Baronet; on his death in 1934 the estates passed to the Tuppers. Lady Wheeler-Cuffe lived at Lyrath House ("to keep the flag flying") until her death in 1962 in her hundredth year.

The day after his relatives departed Wheeler left for the survey at Whirlpool Pass where he and Cautley erected monuments; he then moved on to Fraser Pass where Campbell was doing topographical work. After a brief visit to Banff for a weekend on the Walking Tour and to see Clara off for Sidney, he returned to Jasper where he and Campbell started from Portal Creek for the ascent to Tonquin Valley.

He had a "severe grippy cold" and his temper didn't improve as they rode "the rotten trail, hilly, stony, swampy." But when he arrived everything was "glorious. Not a cloud in the sky." And the view!

From a high station in 1917 he had seen the "south wall and its great icebound escarpments...." Standing on the summit of 7,861-foot Tonquin Hill "the view was magnificent beyond conception": the precipitous Ramparts rising sheer from the valley floor—a striking array of peaks and towers with the formidable mass of Mount Geikie cutting the skyline; and below, "wide, open grassy alpland meadows" jewelled with the Amethyst Lakes. "It is a scene whose memory a lifetime cannot efface."

Though he was sixty-one, life had lost none of its savour. That autumn he journeyed to Assiniboine: "Rode 29 miles today. Not tired." Looking for a camp site for the Club, he and Miss Savatard climbed to Larch Valley and camped in a foot of snow: "Very glorious day. Enjoyed it greatly."

At home in Sidney, he and Clara ushered in the new year at Miss Savatard's cottage where they "drank the families' healths and our own."

On January 3rd word came from "a Los Angeles Undertaking Parlour that Willie had been found dead in his home. Had left directions for burial."

The same day "Granny Macoun very ill." She died a week later. According to the Professor's wishes his body and that of his wife were taken to Ottawa for a funeral at St. Andrew's Presbyterian Church where he "had been an honoured Elder", and they were buried in Beechwood cemetery.

Relieving the burden of grief was the news that Oliver and his wife were on their way home.

Chapter XVII

In March of 1921 Wheeler had received with the greatest excitement the news that Oliver was going on the first expedition to Mount Everest.

In 1849 a trigonometrical survey had established it as earth's highest mountain. For more than half a century attention was focussed on epic attempts to reach the summit of the world; interest was as intense as that created later by landing men on the moon. Situated in a remote and mysterious land, it was forbidden territory for Europeans. Mumm and Longstaff had planned an expedition in 1907. Permission was refused.

In 1921 it was still savagely inaccessible; with its white snow-banner streaming in the wind, it towered in magnificent isolation. Fascinated climbers, explorers, and surveyors had never been closer than sixty miles from its base. To the native people it was a sacred mountain— the mountain "so high no bird can fly over it." It was only after years of delicate diplomatic negotiation that Tibet finally granted permission for the English Alpine Club to send in a reconnaissance expedition.

It is extremely likely that Mumm, Longstaff, and Collie were influential in having Oliver join Colonel Bury's party. His climbing skill and experience, his connection with the Indian army and survey, and his knowledge of photo-topographical survey techinique made him an eminently qualified member. The team, led by Colonel Bury, included another member of the Survey of India, Major Morshead, and the 35-year-old George Leigh Mallory, a gifted mountaineer whose name still has a legendary connection with the great mountain.

Oliver was in camp at Dehra Dun when he received word of his appointment.

"It was a bit of a bombshell, for although I knew that an Expedition had been proposed, I was under the impression that it would not take place until 1922, if at all. And it was with somewhat mixed feelings that I received the news, for I then thought the expedition would leave Darjeeling about the middle of April and I was to be married in Bombay in March! However, it turned out to be not quite so bad as that, and eventually my wife and I reached Darjeeling...on April 30th." At that lovely Indian hill station they had three weeks together before he left for Tibet.

They marched for weeks through lush jungle and on through "the merciless winds of the Tibetan plains." He separated from the party, and with three "high coolies" began his mapping from his base camp on June 24th. For forty-one nights "they slept on moraines and glaciers" at altitudes from eighteen to over twenty-two thousand feet. Unfortunately the weather was "terrible" but he occupied five stations and "got a general idea of the topography." Snowstorms and clouds continued to plague him as he tried for a twenty-thousand foot station, and he returned to headquarters to develop his plates and rest. He then joined Mallory's party in the Rongbuk Valley to map that side of Everest. In all this time he had not seen the summit. But "on the evening of July 23rd it cleared....And what a glorious sight it was!" To Mallory the supreme summit was "...a great white fang excrescent from the jaw-bone of earth. It must be climbed!"

The various parties made extensive journeys of reconnaissance up glaciers and high passes, and at last Mallory decided that the best route of ascent was up the East Rongbuk Glacier and then up a steep wall of snow and ice to a pass, or saddle, more than 22,000 feet high, which he named the North Col. They were not equipped as a climbing party, but Mallory couldn't resist an attempt.

Oliver, Mallory, Bullock, and Morshead established base camp at 17,000 feet, and in a heavy snow storm in mid-September they started out for camp at 19,700 feet. They slept there for two nights and surveyed. Sinking to their knees in soft snow, they plodded upward to "camp at 22,220 feet." It was below zero and the wind howled round their frail tents, but "...with a light cork mattress...a Wolseley valise and a blanket...and our 'flea bags' around us, Bullock and I slept fairly comfortably."

Mallory, Bullock, and Oliver decided to climb on. With snow swirling round the peaks overhead, they continued up the steep slope: "Suffocating eddies of snow just below summit of col...could scarcely stand against wind." They made it to the famous North Col.

Oliver's feet had been completely numb for two hours; Bullock was tired but willing to continue. Oliver thought he could go for another five hundred feet, and Mallory thought they could manage to make it to another thousand feet and hope for better weather. They had "examined the north ridge and [Mallory] saw no technical difficulty of any sort." But they all knew it was really out of the question to tackle the exposed ridge in the full force of the gale. In slow stages they made their way back down.

The difficulties which Mallory dismissed so optimistically cost him his life; he and his young companion disappeared in the mists just below the summit in 1924. No one knows whether they reached the summit.

Oliver lived to see the day when the British team made the first ascent. When the victorious Hillary and Tenzing stood on the roof of the world in 1953 they acknowledged that they had "climbed there on the backs" of those who had so valiantly and persistently tested their skill and strength on the mountain. Millions of dollars had been spent to develop the superb climbing equipment which made that climb possible: the life-giving oxygen in light tanks, feather-weight windproof tents, and down-filled clothing. The first Everest Expedition had equipment and clothing suitable only for climbing in the Alps. Their gallant attempt on the mountain was a remarkable feat.

"Morshead had mapped some twelve thousand square miles of new country on a quarter-inch scale...and I had collected material for the more detailed mapping on the one-inch scale of some six hundred miles in the immediate neighbourhood of Mt. Everest." Those were the first maps of the area and Oliver brought back excellent photographs. They had pioneered the route used by all subsequent attempts to reach Everest from Tibet and established a record by occupying the highest survey station in the world at 22,220 feet. If he hadn't been ill Oliver would certainly have been chosen for the 1922 expedition.

He rejoined his bride five months after leaving. Like Professor Macoun's wife and Clara, Dolly had been initiated into a way of life which included long absences of far-ranging husbands.

In his report Oliver observed: "The bitter winds of Tibet every day from 11 a.m. to 11 p.m. and almost unbroken cloudy weather near Everest... the loneliness when all by myself at high altitudes, waiting and waiting for the clear day that seldom came, all made me long to get back to real trees, comfortable altitudes and civilization. But I would not have missed the 'show' for anything...." How like his father!

With the greatest satisfaction, Wheeler "sent off a screed" about Oliver on Everest to the newspapers and eagerly anticipated his arrival. He was to have a memorable experience himself that year, but meanwhile he went to Banff where he began the season with a flourish.

In the May 24th Regatta on the Bow he was participating happily when his canoe collided with another and Miss Savatard and her companion were thrown overboard. Gallantly, he stood in water to his armpits and rescued the ladies. He hurried home to change but next day had "to go to bed with the grippe."

He had been granted a lease of forty acres in the newly created Assiniboine Provincial Park and permission to build a lodge, and he worked madly, clearing trails to Alpine Club campsites at Palliser and North Kananaskis Passes.

At those camps he performed as vigorously as he had fifteen years before, sending out parties at 5 a.m. and waiting up for a group to return at 4:30 a.m. — "managed to catch two hours sleep before delivering Annual address."

One of the most vital issues discussed was "a proposed scheme to flood a large area of Waterton Lakes Park." He intended to oppose the project and members agreed: "... those parks belong to the people for their benefit and recreation... and not for the purpose of providing dividends for commercial entrepreneurs.... If a National Parks Association does not already exist, one should be formed and the Alpine Club will support it." He lectured in Calgary ("in good form"!) had an interview with an Edmonton paper and "talked into a Radiophone for a while...."

Earlier, when Clara had arrived to preside at Middle Springs, they walked a short distance down the slope to a terraced site he had leased. They had drawn plans for the house they would build there.

It had taken the Topographical Division of the Inter-provincial Boundary Survey nine seasons in the field to trace, monument, and map the watershed from the International Boundary to Yellowhead Pass. Beyond Mount Robson their survey was to be carried through "virtually unknown country." H. F. Lambart of the Geodetic Survey planned to spend the season of 1922 doing a reconnaissance from Yellowhead northwesterly to Jarvis Pass; he had made arrangements with the Royal Canadian Air Force to assist him and his request

A. O. Wheeler and the tiny plane in which he flew around Mount Robson.

that the Force should "extend its facilities to Wheeler" for a flight over the area was granted.

On July 12th Wheeler drove with Lambart and the Jasper Park Superintendent to a small grassy flat near Jasper. There, very near the site of an old fur trading post, stood a fragile bi-plane with a 36 h.p. engine and its pilot from the Air Service Station at High River, Alberta.

Wheeler's initial flight "to get some insight into the method of surveying from an aeroplane" lasted thirty-five minutes and took him up to seven thousand feet. "...for one who has been making maps for the best part of a lifetime, it was a revelation to...gaze upon Nature's map as it unfolded beneath in a slowly moving panorama...although the viewer was travelling at a speed of eighty miles an hour."

Next day he flew "into the heart of the mountain wilderness." Protected only by a narrow windscreen, they took off into low-hanging clouds. Over the Miette Valley, the clouds lifted and lovely lakes gleamed like jewels; at Miette Pass Campbell's tents were a tiny white cluster in a maze of peaks. They swooped near "the mighty mass of Mt. Robson swathed in vapour with great Tumbling Glacier seeming to fall directly from the clouds." At six thousand feet they circled high, snowy Mount Bess and crossed Wolverine Pass, Jackpine River, and Avalanche Pass. Clouds rolled in from the north, and the cold and damp seeped into their bones.

"It is an eerie sensation to be driving at seventy or eighty miles an hour through dense cloud banks, knowing that sheer rock precipices are all around you...." They dropped into a rock-enclosed pocket and the frail craft jolted in the sucking air currents. "It made one think a bit.... It was a queer sensation. I do not think it was fear. When one goes on a trip of that kind on a cloudy day, one should be prepared for any eventuality....But you certainly become thoughtful about possibilities of a forced landing in some unknown and rough-bottomed valley...and if the landing left you alive, you would have to travel for days" to reach food and shelter. His pilot shouted into "the speaking tube" that he might have "to 'pancake' which seemed to mean to stop the engine and let her go until she dropped." They didn't have enough gas to reach Jasper. Losing altitude, they saw a narrow valley, the railway, and a tiny village—and a field of timothy. They landed safely and found they were at McBride, B.C. They "were the first plane ever to land there." Gas was available and amidst the cheering of villagers, they took off. Soon they were flying past "cloud-free Robson, the plane quivering and swaying like a sentient thing."

"I have had the experience of a lifetime! Somehow I felt older...." The apprentice surveyor in birch-bark canoe and Red River cart...nearly a half century ago.... The old surveyor handing over the reins to the eager young generation.

But his professional life *had* spanned the years which were now ushering in the age of aerial photogrammetry, and the thrill of adventure was still strong. "The glorious exhilaration, the boundless space, and the feeling of superiority...." Proudly he was photographed beside the plane in his leather flying suit and lined helmet fastened under his chin. The *Winnipeg Free Press* sent the story and photograph to *The London Times!*

Back in Banff he inspected the Walking Tour where "everything was looking very nice." Striding off from Eau Clair camp on the way back he met Oliver and Dolly. They had been at Sidney with Clara since the first of May. She had written saying "she liked Dolly very much." During the five days together Arthur had an opportunity to get to know his daughter-in-law with her warm cheerful personality and unaffected charm. And it was wonderful to see Oliver being congratulated on his Everest climb. He had splendid photographs which he subsequently showed on a Canadian lecture tour.

On August 16th Wheeler was back in the field for a month. Campbell had been working at Miette, Grant, and Colonel Passes, and Wheeler joined his party at Moose Pass. On the trail "my horse leaped at a creek crossing and tore my breeches all to bits. Did not get hurt." The "boys helped with my tent" and he passed out cigars and candies.

They moved down the Smoky to Chown Creek and to Bess Pass where Wheeler worked high up on the west shoulder of the great mountain. His airplane reconnaissance had helped "to get a general lay of the land"; Lambart's work and Campbell's explorations of the previous season were also most useful, but the weather and travel were execrable. In early September he worked three days at Wolverine Pass, from ten to three each day in "cold, drippy", bleak surroundings. They had to end the season early.

Returning along the Yellowhead, his horse lost its footing in the middle of a stream and he had "to take off my clothes, wring them out and put them on again. Wet." The work accomplished would have been "below average" except for the fact that his 1911 survey made it possible to connect those camera stations with the ones done in 1922.

Oliver and Dolly were in Banff with Clara, and on September 19th they all drove to Calgary where they spent a few pleasant days and then headed for McLeod. "Travel very uninteresting through the flat prairie. McLeod not changed at all." Apparently the terrain he had surveyed thirty years before evoked no nostalgia. The prospect of a long drive on dusty roads through the United States became less tempting with every mile. Impulsively, he decided to return to the fresh clean air at Banff, hoping his family would enjoy their holiday.

This gave him more time for reading the proofs and bringing his Interprovincial Boundary reports up to date and for mailing the photographic plates to the Department. At Sidney he worked in his office and awaited the return of "the motor party" which had spent six weeks at Yellowstone and California. Clara had not been well during the latter part of the holiday and came home by boat. Now that his wife was back, Wheeler took Miss Savatard to a hockey match and back to her home. He spent the night at a hotel and returned to Sidney next morning "in time for a second breakfast with Ol and Dol." Before Christmas he visited Miss Savatard at a Capilano Canyon hotel and they had a long walk; over the fire in the hotel lounge they discussed business—she was consulting him about opening a fancy baking and delicatessen shop.

With Oliver and Dolly and the Everalls, he and Clara spent a happy Christmas; the week's festivities left the young Wheelers tired. Arthur and Clara sat up to see the year of 1923 in alone—"the others asleep."

Oliver had not been well when he returned from India but his leave restored his health. Clara had greatly enjoyed the months spent with them. At the end of February they said good-bye.

With Miss Savatard busy in her shop (she didn't go to Banff the next summer), Miss Rowland, the Wheeler's housekeeper, helped in the office and often accompanied Arthur on the long walks he loved; occasionally she and a friend and Miss Savatard enjoyed evenings with him at the theatre and sometimes Clara joined them. In the spring she was well enough to work in her garden.

But her sister, Nellie Everall, was gravely ill. Arthur had visited her regularly at Resthaven and did so just before he left for Banff. He never saw her again.

Chapter XVIII

In June he and Clara inspected the construction of their house in Banff, and before she began a busy season at Middle Springs camp, at the clubhouse, and overseeing the house building, they celebrated their thirty-fifth wedding anniversary on June 6th. They canoed to his favourite picnic spot on the Bow and had a special treat in the village ice-cream parlour in the evening. "Glorious day."

Two weeks later he was in Jasper, expecting to take an additional pack-train to the field. Campbell had already taken in one outfit, as their work would be in remote country and a cache for supplies had to be established halfway, at Colonel Pass. Campbell unexpectedly arrived back in Jasper; in flooded creeks he had lost a load of supplies and eight horses had strayed away. He was able to take Wheeler's horses and supplies back in. As travel was difficult, it would take Campbell considerable time to reach the field of operations, so Wheeler returned for a short flurry of activity in Banff.

He distributed his Walking Tour circulars at Glacier House, Emerald Lake, Lake Louise Chateau, and Sicamous—all the hostesses met him "with open arms"—and made a brisk survey of camps and trails. "Sunshine Camp dirty and unattractive. Fired Robinson and gave him a bad talking too"! Alpine Club camp was staked out and tents brushed; "fired two men for being lazy." At the Larch Valley Camp the Director again spoke about the urgency of organizing a National Parks Association. The meeting declared itself in favour and an organizational meeting of the Canadian National Parks Association was held immediately.

Wheeler returned to Banff, where Clara was still living at Middle Springs, and on August 5th she "came up to the clubhouse to spend the afternoon and have supper" with him. On the 6th, "a dull, cold day, Clara came up in the afternoon and saw me off at the clubhouse."

Back in the field, he was following the Smoky River, making his way over Bess Pass and Jackpine Valley—"the worst trail I know; marsh, rocks, and holes." Cautley and Lambart in separate parties were locating the boundary along the 120th Meridian. The Topographical Division under Mr. Campbell had worked well under difficult conditions. Having cut trails up the valley of Meadowland Creek, where Wheeler joined them, they moved camp to Loren Lake Pass, Jones Pass, and Beaverdam Pass.

On August 23rd and 24th Wheeler was waiting for clinging clouds to lift so that he could climb at Avalanche Pass. On the 25th a man left for Jasper to. replenish supplies, and on Sunday the 26th Wheeler climbed, but clouds hung like shrouds and he came down. At three o'clock the next afternoon the weather cleared and he was ready to climb when the man arrived back from Jasper with a letter from his good friend, Mrs. Brewster. "Clara very ill. Must come at once."

For three days he travelled as quickly as bad trails allowed. As he approached the railway near Robson a messenger met him with a wire. "Clara died 5:30 a.m. August 24th. Woe is me!"

She had collapsed August 23rd and the wire had been sent to the Brewsters immediately.

On the train from Jasper he cabled Oliver and wrote to Miss Savatard; in Calgary he found that their old friend Dean Paget was away. He wired Club Secretary Mitchell to arrange the funeral for Monday, September 3rd.

"Got some roses, a black tie and some crepe." Alpine Club friend, T. G. Moffat, sat with him on the train to Banff. "Croft met me and drove me to the morgue. Saw my dear dead girl and placed roses on her."

The bleak Sunday he "spent aimlessly at Middle Springs", the camp where she had worked so hard. In her tent-house, just as she had left them, were her personal possessions—and the presence of her absence.

The day after the funeral he visited the little cemetery. The mound of broken brown earth was covered with wilting and dying flowers. He sat for a long time in the sun and listened to the icy river softly whispering on its rocky bed.

Days passed before he could face the visit to Claremount. There he found the brass rods for the new curtains, her unpacked trunks.... For most of their married life he had been away six months of the year. Now, with his work diminishing, they would have been together here.

Oliver and Dolly came October 13th. They visited Clara's grave and helped Arthur pack her things for shipment to Sidney. They drove home, stopping a few days at the ranch of their friends, the MacCarthy's, at Wilmer. Arthur went by train, stopping on the way home at Harrison Hot Springs for a day with Miss Savatard; together they visited her married sister, Sybil Gee, at Ruskin for a day.

As soon as he arrived home, he and Miss Rowland walked to the cemetery to place flowers on Nellie's grave. Arthur had been devoted to her. Strangely, she and Clara, who had a very warm relationship, died almost simultaneously. Nellie was dying of cancer. Within minutes of Clara's death she came out of a long coma, and family members insisted that she had said quite distinctly: "I'm coming, Clara." She died without regaining consciousness.

With Oliver and Dolly present, social life resumed and Oliver revived his father's interest in plans for an expedition to climb Canada's highest peak, Mount Logan. On November 29th the young couple had to leave for India.

In February, on the way to a meeting of Boundary Commissioners in Edmonton, Wheeler stopped off at Banff to visit Clara's grave and walked up to look again at Claremount. A few years later, writing to a friend similarly bereaved, he said: "Go to the mountains; they are the great comforters. I have been through the experience. I know."

Travelling from Jasper to Robson in June, he remembered the words of the great mountaineer, A. F. Mummery: "Happily for us the great brown slabs bending over into immeasurable space, the lines and curves of the wind-moulded cornices, the delicate undulations of fissured snow, are old and trusted friends, ever luring us to fun and laughter and enabling us to bid a sturdy defiance to all the ills that time and life oppose."

The Club camp was at Robson that year. Rising early to rouse climbers, he looked up at Robson's white majesty soaring above Berg Lake. The air was clean, dew-washed and the solitude was enhanced by the haunting, ululating cry of the loon. His vigour and zest returned.

In late August he was working with Cautley and Lambart at Robson Pass and climbed the slope of Mount Mumm, where a brass bolt marks the straight line survey of the Pass. Travelling to Sheep Creek was "very interesting. New country for me". In Campbell and Cautley's camp he again handed out candies and cigars; on the way his "horse and outfit took a swim", and he had spent hours drying out these treats for his men.

They had worked from Caskat Pass to Mount Torrens, occupying over seventy camera stations. Since 1918 Cautley's division had surveyed and monumented the boundary along the 120th Meridian; by then it had become clear that Wheeler's work from Howse to Robson Pass would cover the most rugged and inaccessible section of the Continental Divide and take several seasons; Cautley's men, therefore, proceeded with the work on the Meridian. From Sheep Creek camp Wheeler participated in locating the watershed over a ridge of Intersection Mountain— fifty feet west of this point the 120th Meridian intersects the Divide and thereafter the Meridian becomes the boundary.

There was only one more pass to ascend. On the way to Miette Pass, it rained and snowed dismally. wheeler was plagued with a toothache for days. Still, there were "the comfy camps"! On the last few miles of the trail the September snows fell in blinding sheets and the horses floundered in three foot drifts, but he and Cautley stayed on to complete the location for monument sites. The map work would take another two years but the field work was finished.

Did he think for a moment of all the other passes he had crossed in the last twelve years? The sinuous line of the watershed covers nearly 750 miles. He and his men had travelled on foot and on horseback to reach the passes and the stations and return; many sites had to be re-visited—the total mileage must have run into thousands. It was the most comprehensive project to which the technique of photo-topography had ever been applied. For the methods available at the time it was a massive undertaking.

With his sense of occasion he had arranged for a ceremony to commemorate the completion of the survey. Very appropriately the site was Robson Pass. It was in 1911, when he had made the critical decision to continue his work in the Rockies, that he had in effect initiated the Interprovincial Survey in this area.

The Alpine Club of Canada was on hand for the unveiling of the special monument: "The work of the boundary survey has been of very special interest and benefit to the Club and its widely scattered members... As the boundary... lies along the crests of the highest peaks of the Rockies... the mapping of these areas and distribution of information has been of great value to all visitors and prospective visitors to the Canadian Rockies.... Map distribution in connection with the boundary survey has greatly surpassed original expectations and many sheets... have gone through several editions...."

On July 31st members of the English, American, Appalachian, French, and Swiss Alpine Clubs joined the Surveyor General of British Columbia, the Deputy Minister of Lands for the province, J. N. Wallace, and C.N.R. and C.P.R. executives on the summit of Robson Pass between Berg and Adolphus Lake. As a tribute to the invaluable work of Wheeler's assistant, A. J. Campbell, Mrs. Campbell was given the honour of unveiling the memorial monument. Its brass plate "recorded the name of the late Edouard Deville... who introduced to Canada the method of phototopographical surveying, a method so well suited to her mountain regions and so successfully carried on in mapping them. It is fitting that his name should be on record at a place where their grandeur reaches a climax.

"The ceremony was an impressive one. The towering, magnificence of mighty snow-clad Mt. Robson... gave solemnity and dignity to the scene.... The great mountain, whose crest, golden in the fitful sunshine and then obscured by passing clouds, was a full mile above us; close by, the glorious blue waters of Berg and Adolphus Lakes, and all round, wide-spreading snowfields, icefalls and precipitous rock ramparts.... It brought home to us the magnitude of the works of Nature... and the wonderful heritage we possess in this mountain wilderness of unsurpassed scenic splendour."

The Union Jack which draped the monument was withdrawn and the guests hurried to camp for lunch. A. O. Wheeler remained beside the ceremonial stone to be photographed: stocky, grey-bearded, climbing boot firmly planted on the rock, his face composed and serious—his eyes focussed on the distant horizon.

On the train journey to Edmonton and Calgary he had many glimpses of the serrated ranges which close the western skyline. Beyond those outer peaks towered "the big ones". There his "stone men" marking the line would endure. At sixty-four, was there just a hint of nostalgia? A rewarding career was about to end.

But he had another matter on his mind. In August he had written Oliver about Miss Savatard. He wrote very formally to her father asking for Emmeline's hand in marriage. The Reverend Mr. Savatard replied and also sent a letter to his daughter, saying he had read Mr. Wheeler's request with tears in his eyes and beseeched her to devote her life to being a good wife. It is surprising that this iron-jawed cleric was capable of such tender sentiments.

In Edmonton Wheeler bought pyjamas for "Ems" and in Calgary, "ordered ring to be ready by the 12th." Staying at Miss Mollison's there, he had a long chat with his old friend who "was sympathetic". He stopped in Banff to visit the cemetery. At Golden he got the marriage licence and booked a room at the hotel in the tiny village of Salmon Arm.

"Put in balance of day as best I could." He was as restless and nervous as a bridegroom of twenty!

Next day he caught the early train to Salmon Arm and "saw Mrs. Sterling. Made arrangements for wedding tomorrow. Got in touch with Reverend Wheeler." (Not a relative, but a minor coincidence). On October 8th he met her at the train and took her to the hotel. "Bought drinks.... At 11:55 a.m." they were married in the tiny Anglican church. "Went to Mrs. Sterling's and drank the health of the bride!"

They went to Sicamous and took a boat to a beach camp. The lake reflected the softly wooded hills with their sombre green and brilliant autumn colouring. By their solitary firelight they "opened May's [Monks] boxes. A beautiful cake, very weddingy and a bottle of Benedictine". They ate their wedding supper, "blessed May and drank our healths." He made "a very comfy camp and a delightful bed of boughs".

This became "Honeymoon Camp" to which they returned year after year.

For ten lazy days they fished and sailed on the Shuswap Lakes. On their return to Banff they went immediately to Clara's grave and planted the Oregon grape and juniper they had gathered at the Lakes. In Victoria they bought a "Victrola" and when they arrived at Sidney, neighbours had "everything bright and comfy. Victrola concert by the fire in the evening."

They took up their social life with old friends and just as he had always kept in very close touch with all his relatives, he now added the Savatards to his list; the Rev. Mr. Savatard received Christmas gifts and Sybil Savatard Gee and her husband were Christmas guests, as well as Nellie Macoun Everall's husband and daughter, Eleanor. As a wedding gift Lady Charlotte Wheeler-Cuffe sent a valuable painting. Their former housekeeper, Miss Rowland, who had been so kind at the time of Clara's death, received as her gift Arthur's photograph.

Before the new year: "Cable from Oliver. Son and heir!"

Chapter XIX

At the Robson camp's annual meeting, Wheeler announced his intention to resign as Director. He felt conditions had changed and "the Club would benefit if new blood was introduced." He was given a vote of confidence by the meeting: "President Patterson, in a moving address to younger members, paid tribute to the Director's many years of service—the Club's success was due to his executive powers, enthusiasm, firmness and warm geniality." It had "been a work of love for which he received no remuneration whatever."

The organization had played a vigorous role in the organization of the Canadian National Parks Association, which the President believed "would come to be regarded as one of the Club's finest achievements."

Wheeler certainly pursued this work energetically; there was concern about Calgary Power's planned development at Spray Lakes. He sent articles to newspapers across Canada; one cartoon showed avaricious coal, electrical power, timber, and mining entrepreneurs lopping off great sections of valuable National Park land. In a published Edmonton interview, speaking as a member of the C.N.P.A., he outlined their stand: "...the National parks must be maintained for the use of the people and their heirs, free from entry by any commercial interests....I am opposed to the Spray Lakes scheme for the reason that it will establish precedent, and as such, establish unanswerable argument for an application of any kind in any of the parks that might be considered necessary for commercial interests. The Alpine Club opposes the scheme for the same reason."

When he was in the East in 1925 he took the matter up with the Commissioner of Parks. The organization's efforts were in vain. They were in fact a half century before their time. The vital importance of preserving the natural environment wasn't realized, nor was any effective action taken, until 1972.

He still worked in his office but when the three beautiful atlases which accompanied the Interprovincial Boundary volumes were complete, he received only "a superannuation of $62 a month" from the Department. So while he was in the East he saw Murray Gibbon, Publicity Manager for the C.P.R. and reached an agreement to produce large maps of mountain areas to display in the Company's mountain hotels and bungalow camps. Alan Thomson produced the maps and Wheeler paid him two-thirds of the amount received. "Spike" Thomson had to take a very strong stand to get this share. Wheeler had insisted on less. Although he was by no means as wealthy as "Lockie" Hamilton who had made a fortune in real estate, he had invested astutely in Victoria property and securities and enjoyed a comfortable retirement income.

The trip East had been arranged as a family reunion to introduce his wife. With great interest he helped her buy a fine new hat and clothes for the occasion. They went first to the Rectory in Peterborough to see Joey. Because she was the youngest, this sister received an extra share of the paternal interest that Wheeler took in the family after the death of his father. Perhaps she was also his favourite because they were remarkably alike in temperament. She had a gracious and hospitable manner and a great deal of spirit which sometimes manifested itself in fiery outbursts of temper. The flash would die quickly and she could never understand why anyone should not forgive and forget as she did. She was, however, too proud to actually apologize for hurting anyone's feelings, but would proffer a little gift instead. Possibly she and her brother also got on so well because they were not often together.

Uncle Arthur was a great favourite and enjoyed himself immensely; he bought his nephews "air pistols and icecreams". Had he known that the boys "who were not about to tarnish the reputation for mischief attributed to sons of clergymen" went around taking pot-shots at neighbouring houses, they would have been treated to "a stiff talking to"!

Joey and her husband went with them to visit all the Hamiltons in Collingwood. His sister Kathleen had died in Ottawa in 1924. Unhappily, Kathleen received very little encouragement for the intellectual bent she inherited from the Helsham side of the family, but her literary efforts helped her to maintain some degree of independence. When in her mid-twenties a suitor appeared, Mrs. Wheeler forbade the marriage; the widower married his housekeeper and when she died in 1914 Kathleen had married him. It was not a happy marriage.

Arthur and his wife then went to "Willie's farm" (the Ottawa Experimental Farm), and when Oliver and Dolly arrived, "Saw the boy. A *very* fine baby." John Oliver Wheeler, his grandson.

Wheeler lectured on the way home, and Oliver, Dolly, and John Oliver awaited them on their return to Sidney where they brought gaiety and initiation into a new era.

Oliver took his father to look at automobiles, and tentatively they brought home a stately and ornate Essex for a weekend trial. "Oliver gave me first lesson in theory of Motor Cars." Oliver continued these instructions "re the theory of Motor Cars" daily for two weeks; A. O. then "practiced steering.... Making some progress...exercising with the car every day." Mastery seemed at hand and he sallied forth to Patricia Bay; on his return, "Hit the gate and stalled. No damage except fence and gate." He went into the ditch next day on the same route but managed to get "into the garage in good shape." At last, in high triumph: "Drove all hands including the baby over to Gales for tea." There was confidence! Risking his grandson's life. And indeed, it was fortunate that cars were made of sturdier stuff in those days, for driving with A. O. continued to be a hair-raising experience. He didn't *drive* a car. He *rode* it. After all, he had spent more than half a century in a saddle.

Another innovation was the radio. With Oliver and Dolly in the house, "radio going evenings. Jazz." And instead of walking to the drug store where

The road to Golden via the Kicking Horse Canyon, typical of the British Columbia roads which A. O. Wheeler navigated in his Essex.

men assembled to hear the all-important Stanley Cup hockey finals, he could now enjoy them at home, although "the static" was often irritating, having a way of coming at most crucial moments. An evening at the movies seeing Charlie Chaplin in "The Gold Rush" and Will Rogers in "So this is London" provided "lots of laughs". All too soon it was time for "Ol, Dolly and Co." to leave for India again.

The licence plates for his Essex were number 1066 and henceforth all his cars were christened "Old Bill" after William the Conqueror! "Old Bill" (and Ems' nerves) were put to the test that summer. They went on a motoring and camping trip to Cameron Lake to celebrate his birthday. On the first morning he got up to make breakfast with the new gasoline camp stove. In spite of reading the directions with care, there ensued a "Circus with camp stove. Saved the tent from catching fire." On the way home they "got mired". Nonetheless, they drove to Banff via Washington, Bonner's Ferry, Cranbrook, and the newly opened road from Windermere over Vermilion Pass. It took eight days. In September, on the return journey, on a "gumbo road three miles from Creston the car nearly skidded over the 200-foot precipice. Saved by a miracle. No gravel or guard rail." In snow, "Old Bill" was negotiated round "steep crooked curves and switchbacks near Grand Forks" and the only casualty was a smashed oil tank: "hit rock".

The perils of motoring were very real in those days; any doubt is dispelled by glancing at old photos of the mountain roads of the time. But he had travelled over much worse terrain on horseback, and he doggedly and confidently persisted — it was just a new challenge. In spite of being hauled from glutinous ditches with horses and bemoaning smashed fenders on the drive from Salmon Arm to Victoria, he was ecstatic: "The end of a most thrilling drive of 514 miles"!

At Banff, in the spring, he had worked briskly on his Assiniboine Tours. He enjoyed some exhilarating tramps and rides, but by 1927 conditions were changing. He and two men took patrons by pack-train to Crowsnest Pass; "the trail was bad. Much cutting to do... very hard on men and horses." An excursion to Jasper was successful eventually, but going via Howse Pass, he complained that the horses "were cripples" — and one drowned in the Blaeberry and one just "lay down and died." He was over-extending himself and his resources, now that he no longer had the experienced surveyor-travellers to supplement his staff. If the riding and walking tours were to survive they required a more extensive organization.

As soon as he had the tours well established he unsuccessfully petitioned the Federal Government to take them over. But the Canadian Pacific Railway could see the potential. Their Director of Publicity, J. Murray Gibbon, consulted Wheeler about trails; and the maps Wheeler made for the Company were always marked with any new trails.

A colourful Russian-Italian nobleman, Nicholas degli Albizzi, a superb skier who had been a war hero in charge of a regiment of Alpine troops in the Tyrol, had become enchanted with Mount Assiniboine as a centre for skiing. He began making tentative approaches to Wheeler to buy his interests. With the subsequent interest of a very famous and handsome young Norwegian skier, Erling Strom, a complex partnership was formed with the C.P.R. Over a period of years Strom bought out Wheeler's interest at Assiniboine. Gibbon used the immense resources of the C.P.R. to give world-wide publicity to what became the very popular Trail Riders of the Canadian Rockies and The Skyline Trail Hikers. Wheeler had laid the plans and his original dream was fulfilled — thousands still come each year to enjoy the high trails.

In 1926 the tents of the Alpine Club were pitched below the austere Ramparts of the Tonquin Valley; beside the flickering campfire, A. O. Wheeler delivered his last address as Director. Appropriately, 80-year-old Professor Fay, who had encouraged his early efforts to form the Club, was present. The Director's position was replaced by a Committee of Management; and Wheeler was elected Honourary President.

A. L. Mumm wrote: "If ever a man was entitled to lay down an office with the consciousness that he had accomplished a memorable and unique work, it was you.... I can't think of anyone who has accomplished quite such a bit of constructive work in the cause of mountaineering as you have done.... Some day I hope to write something about this and you will find yourself on an appropriately lofty pedestal." He also referred amusingly to the grumbling he had heard about "the Crusty Old Director".

Longstaff also wrote, noting that "...it is not likely that younger members know or appreciate what the Club owes you."

His habit of autocratic directing had caused friction—a new generation was anxious to take over the reins which he had perhaps held too firmly and too long. Ever since Robson had been won he had been urging an expedition to Mount Logan, Canada's highest mountain. In 1925 when he served as an official of the committee in charge of the expedition there was trouble. At one point he resigned from it but cooler heads restored harmony and he reconsidered. However, hurt pride didn't diminish his high triumph when friends Lambart and MacCarthy led the party which made the first ascent.

He continued to send out profuse press releases about Alpine Club activities (which "Ems typed beautifully"— and how keenly he looked for errors!) solicited C.P.R. and government assistance, selected and recommended campsites, prepared camp circulars, and sent his annual anniversary greeting to members.

It 1929 camp was again at Rogers Pass and with Ems and sister Joey, he tramped to some of his old survey camps. Sitting on a log to rest, he fell off and cracked two ribs. This didn't prevent him from going on an expedition a month later.

He had named a striking mountain near the junction of the Alexandra and Saskatchewan River for his English Alpine Club friend, Leopold S. Amery. Ever since his trip to Robson with Hastings, Mumm, and Inderbinen, Amery had longed to return to the Rockies. In 1929 he decided to come and climb "his" mountain. Making arrangements for the eminent visitor (he was Secretary of State for the Colonies), the C.P.R.'s Murray Gibbon realized that the trip would be enhanced by Wheeler's presence. With Swiss guide Edouard Feuz, Amery succeeded and met "the challenge to prove myself as a mountaineer."

He was delighted to be reunited with Wheeler and never forgot him "as my comrade on the long expedition, [who was] at the age of sixty-nine, ever the first up in camp and busiest with the packing; tireless on the longest day and the first busy with cutting tent poles and bedding and with putting up tents on arrival in camp. His only complaint was that two cracked ribs...prevented active high-level climbing!" This was partly natural zest for camp life but it is also the Wheeler of tradition carrying out the obligations and pleasures of host. Naturally, he sent accounts to all newspapers.

Each autumn when they closed Claremount in Banff, he and Ems celebrated their wedding anniversary at Sicamous. Trout suppers (how proud he was of Ems' fishing prowess, although her efforts were invariably spurred on by spirited and firm advice!) tramping on the beach, lazily trolling and sailing, "glorious moonlight nights", lights and shadows on the lake, autumn's radiance on wooded hills—all became imperishable memories.

In 1929 they drove down the coast to California, spending Christmas en route in a tourist cabin. For three months they enjoyed beach picnics with friends and relatives, the Rose Bowl Tournament, and New Year's Eve "seeing the lights of Hollywood and Los Angeles." But even here the morning hours were spent on personal and Canadian National Parks correspondence and preparing illustrated lectures which he delivered to the Los Angeles Nature Club and the Sierra Club. All along the route down he had inquired at likely places where he might show off the beauties of the Canadian Rockies.

On the way home "the Redwoods Highway scenery magnificent!" As soon as they arrived in Banff he hurried to Calgary to buy plants to fix Clara's grave. Although there was now (as he had advocated long years before) an Information Bureau for visitors in Banff, many tourists still called at Claremount for information. And there was always the pleasure of welcoming Alpine Club friends.

In 1930 they took the train to Jasper and journeyed to camp at Maligne Lake. He took charge of the tents housing the party of British Columbia's Lieutenant Governor: "Brushed the beds." The last few days he was in bed with "a grippy cold"; the distinguished visitor called and "left a bottle of liquid gold" to soothe his thoughtful host.

In 1931, when he was seventy-one, he spent "glorious days" measuring the Illecillewaet and Victoria Glaciers. He and Ems walked from Moraine Lake to O'Hara camp. They were on the trail from 10:30 until 8:30 in the evening: "Hard going. Pretty tired." Nonetheless, a few weeks later he was measuring the Robson Glacier: "Morning view of Mt. Robson superb." The results of these studies were included in a paper for the International Commission on Glaciers, which was held in 1931.

In September he and Ems went on horseback to look over the campsite for next year. Their horses got away during the night on the homeward trip and they walked home "from Canmore Gap" to Banff. At seventy-two he drove from their idyllic Shuswap holiday over Vermilion Pass in a blinding snowstorm. The car skidded off the road and they had to wait for "a wrecker". It was shortly after this that he began carrying a flask of whisky — a temperate draught helped to fortify him against these arduous "motor tours".

At the end of November 1932 they hurried home from Sicamous to a great flurry of preparation. On Armistice Day "Oliver, Dolly and Co." arrived. A. O. Wheeler hadn't seen his son and grandson for seven years. What a delight to show "John Oliver my lantern slides"! He and John walked to put the usual wreath on Nellie's grave and cut their Christmas tree. The house was decorated on Christmas day and the reunited family and friends enjoyed "Jolly Christmas dinner".

The winter trip to California was a family one that year — the five of them were together for three months. On their return he and Ems hurried to Banff to ready Claremount for Ol and Dolly, and on the train a few days later, "John Oliver arrived in style". Oliver, Dolly, and John attended Club camp in Paradise Valley where A. O., his costume enhanced with neckerchief and colourful woollen toque, presided at the campfire with his old flair.

Conrad Kain was at Camp and spoke at an evening campfire. Wheeler noted: "Made fool of himself. Pretty full. Turned in myself before he was finished".

He was disgusted with this unseemly behaviour. He didn't sense that Conrad, a sentimental man, was overcome with nostalgia and the premonition that it might be his final camp. He died a few months later.

When Wheeler saw Oliver and Dolly off at the end of August, he wrote in his diary: "I wonder if I shall ever see them again."

At home in Sidney he began cleaning out his office — crates of records were turned over to the Surveyor General of British Columbia. He sold his old survey tent and outfit and looked over diaries to write an article about his Riel Rebellion experiences. With Ems away on a long holiday in England, he was lonely and thoughtful. Eleanor Everall had a surprise party for his seventy-seventh birthday, to which neighbours brought "a cake and home brew". Always convivial, he enjoyed himself immensely, but a few days later he "wrote note to W. G. Hamilton re my possible death."

Oliver and Dolly had made arrangements for John to be educated in Canada. (They returned themselves to live in Windermere Valley when Oliver retired in 1947.) As guardian to his grandson, A. O. now took a renewed interest in his family heritage. "Took John Oliver to become Canadian citizen. Race, nationality Irish."!

"Wrote Joey re family lineage papers." His interest intensified when he received word of Sir Otway Wheeler-Cuffe's death. He may have entertained the idea that he could inherit the peerage. But rules restrict the inheritance of a Baronetcy—it cannot be passed on to a cousin. The Wheeler-Cuffe Baronetcy became extinct in 1934 simply because there was no one to inherit in the manner set out, and the Lyrath property passed to the Tuppers.

John's presence in Banff relieved his loneliness—together they went to Assiniboine: "Rode 20 miles first day. Glad to turn in." He was absent from Alpine Club camp and sent officials his typed annual address. But it was a great pleasure to take John to the Skyline Trail Hikers' "pow wow and present him as youngest member."

Ems returned in August and the three of them enjoyed the Shuswap holiday, sleeping in the open under a canopy of stars, sitting by the evening fire and watching distant lightning. "John had fine time climbing rocks, boating...." Emulating his grandfather, he took over morning tasks. "John lighted fire at 5:30 a.m." and brought them tea in bed. Next morning he began chores at 4:15, and on the next he was ready to start "at 2:30 a.m."

As the days closed in softly and the September moon rose over the hills, John would ask for more tales "of the good old days"—the reminiscing brought equal pleasure to the pioneer surveyor and his grandson. He "introduced him to the science of surveying" by constructing a crude plane-table. Next day: "John happily surveying and mapping....Wrote Ol enclosing John's map of Weasel Cove." After two weeks he was taken to town for a haircut and they put him on the train "with six companions and a Master". John was going to Shawinigan Lake School on Vancouver Island. He was home for Christmas holidays, of course, and more than ever the Wheeler house was lively, filled with children.

A. O. had real affection for children which was reciprocated. One of the most pleasant memories of a niece was of holidays spent at the Sidney house. Each morning she would be wakened by a freshly shaven, clean-smelling Uncle Arthur with a delightfully "whiskery kiss". He loved walks on the beach, picnics, games, and going to the woods to gather wild flowers with them. And now, special parties for John and his friends: "Good time. Plenty noise!"

Ushering in 1935, there were great plans for a party at which "John O is going to lecture." They spent days picking out the best slides from Grandfather's collection (during which John was undoubtedly the recipient of much advice on the techniques of lecturing), and the event was a great success. His friends and their mothers came to tea and the lecture "lasted fifty minutes!"

A.O. and Ems went for their California holidays in a luxury liner that year. It was pleasant to sit in the sun and watch the planes taking off at Burbank airfield. And a friend took him for a drive in his new "...Terraplane. Went 80 m.p.h.! Thrilling!" They drove south for the next two winters; when he was seventy-seven he had "slammed into a hillside" on the way where the roads were wet and slippery with slushy snow. In spite of rising at five on the homeward journey to drive "270 miles" in one day on "poor winding roads", he still had time to enjoy the Washington scenery: "Very picturesque. Magnificent views!"

Coming home from their 1935 Shuswap holiday, "Old Bill" had slithered into a ditch near Cranbrook on "rotten road, boulders, gravel and dust in clouds. One tire destroyed, broken spring, running board beyond repair." While the car was towed out and the tire changed, he and Ems went "up town and had a beer." And on the same drive when he was seventy-eight, he "stopped to let a car pass. It struck me....On Lookout Mt. had bad skid. Nearly went over fall of several hundred feet."

At Banff, life was more serene. In the garden behind Claremount he had piped water from Middle Springs and constructed his own sulphur pool. His niece, Eleanor Everall Sanderson, recalls seeing him "sally forth each morning, looking like a mountain dryad...an all-pink one with white hair, beard and towel-wrapped middle."

Another niece, Mrs. Hester Hughes, remembers that "He seemed happiest at their Banff home [which] sat in the loveliest four acres I had ever seen. They had cleared out only the rank weeds, leaving the lovely native flowers to flourish....And the pool where "he would crouch and bounce in the water up to his neck, puffing, blowing bubbles and chortling....Unless the bear got to the pond first; in that case we wisely waited our turn."

When asked if she remembered him, Mrs. Hughes replied: "Indeed I do, because of a continuing influence on a budding life..." Of their Sidney home, where she spent Easter vacations from the time when she was ten until she was sixteen, she said: "...everything in the household moved with dignified precision under his firm hand. Every morning they arose at 7 a.m. and precisely at 8 we were seated for breakfast; Uncle Arthur, ruddy-shaven and impeccable always, in his white shirt, tie, Norfolk jacket, puttees and ankle boots. The unvarying routine continued with his leaving for the office, an empty house they owned on the street 'out back'. Here were his hundreds of rolled maps, many suspended from the ceiling, a hugh surveyor-type drawing-board desk...There, he also had a hugh correspondence, almost world-wide...and when I think that he wrote every word in his precision longhand, I deplore and pity the sluggards of today.

"Following the 'wee nap' after lunch, the afternoons were generally devoted to my entertainment-instruction. After dinner we would play Spillikens'— a game in which one tried to remove one match from a huge pile without moving another, all with the aid of a piece of kindling whittled down to a fine point. This too was a ritual, giving each common task its due dignity and importance. The great bumps on each of his finger joints must have been painful, yet he would take his fine-pointed 'lifter' and sneak up to the matches with the control and delicacy of an artisan. As a final fillip to the evening, he would go to the portable Victrola, ceremoniously take a record from its jacket, just as ceremoniously dust it off with a special brush, place the record reverently on the machine and sit back just as if he were in a loge at the theatre....

"I wrote to him regularly and he would answer...always correcting the letters, *never* with haughty authority—I always felt a worthwhile person in his presence—but so that I would grow. If my letters were correct, a dime would fall out. Oh, happy day—an accolade from Uncle Arthur."

She remembers also another innovation at Claremount, "...which had a 'wee house' in the most impractical but poetic spot. Back of the house the path turned at the woodshed (practical thus far), crossed the hot spring by a tiny bridge and continued over a flowered pathway into the first of the woods. Now this was quite a trek for such a necessary terminal, so to avoid waste of time and possible embarrassment, on a corner of the woodshed in full sight of the kitchen windows, the British Flag was nobly waving on a spindle: UP for occupied, DOWN for vacant."

At that woodpile he still worked, carefully measuring each stick to make sure he had not been cheated by the tradesman! Ems had friends in the village and attended the little Anglican Church, St. George's in the Pines, while he gathered and arranged bouquets of wildflowers. There was always a bowl of these under Clara's portrait. And on birthdays, he placed sprays of fir over "family portraits".

In 1938 another photograph was added. Since 1936 he had corresponded with Irish solicitors and Lady Wheeler-Cuffe about Bishop Jonas Wheeler's Elizabethan flagon. When the eighteenth century Wheelers presented it to the Cathedral Church of St. Canice, they had a copy made which was kept at Lyrath House. It is extremely likely that he pressed his case with Lady Wheeler-Cuffe, hoping that the copy flagon would be left to his family on her death. He failed.

It would be appropriate for the venerable flagon to be in the Wheeler's possession, but an equally good case can be made for keeping it at the ancient estate at Lyrath. The piece his family has, Mrs. Wheeler's Communion cup/chalice, is an exquisite companion piece made of the same cocoanut, and Lady Cuffe did send him a photograph of the Lyrath Flagon.

Visitors to Claremount now saw, tastefully displayed, the photograph, the Communion cup, die stamps of the Wheeler Crest, and his Riel Rebellion mementoes: Saskatchewan Medal and clasp, an old felt hat with a red flannel band, a pair of spurs, a buffalo powder horn and bayonet. And a splendidly-crafted loonskin bag, commemorating Professor Macoun's pioneering journeys.

Chapter XX

When he sat on his verandah at Claremount, looking down on the thousands of cars thronging to the mountains he had the satisfaction of knowing that he had been empire building too. He had once referred to Alpine Club members as "empire builders"; not as builders of personal empires but in the sense of opening this "rich resource... acting as its custodian and passing it on as a sure heritage for generations to come."

He hadn't amassed a fortune, however, and during the depression years he worried about money. He sold property he had acquired years before in Victoria. His nagging concern was that he might not be able to leave a legacy large enough to keep Ems living in some comfort after his death.

His relationship with her was one of tender devotion — in notes accompanying gifts to her he invariably expressed the wish that he could have given her the more expensive ones she deserved. However, in spite of necessary economies, he continued to order his "Norfolk coat and breeches" (tweed with a slightly green tinge) from his London tailors.

In the summer of 1937 Oliver and Dolly arrived in Banff with John. Club camp was in the Yoho Valley — the site of the first camp thirty-one years before. It was a proud moment for father and grandfather when John did his graduating climb on Mount President.

The holidays continued at Shuswap where Oliver and Dolly had rented a launch. One day grandson John saw an example of pioneer initiative in emergencies. "Ems got in hornets' nest and received painful stings. Applied brown sugar, carbonate of soda, peroxide and Chase's ointment. Effective."!

Oliver and Dolly helped them celebrate their thirteenth anniversary at Claremount where "Ems put up a fine dinner. Ice cream and drinks...." His delight in her culinary accomplishments was always recorded in the diaries. And how he loved the convivial cup, and with what gusto he pronounced his customary "Cheers all round!" There was a very special ceremony for John's birthday in Sidney. His parents saw A.O. present him with Clara's 1906 ice axe. Oliver and Dolly accompanied them to California and on April 2nd, 1938, they said good-bye.

The ravaging pain of arthritis became more severe, and often he "spent whole day trying to find comfortable position" in bed. In Banff it now took a whole day to plant the flowers on Clara's grave.

But sister Joey came to brighten the summer of 1939. King George VI and Queen Elizabeth were making a Canadian tour and stayed at the Banff Springs Hotel. A.O. was up early decorating the car with Union Jacks and buntings and they left Claremount in good time to get a choice location on the royal route. As their Majesties' drove slowly by, waving in their customary manner, the Queen noticed a dignified, bearded old Edwardian gentleman doffing his hat and bowing most graciously. She turned round and looked directly at him and gave him a special smile and prolonged wave. Joey was extremely proud!

The habit, developed over the years, of spending morning hours in the office continued but the work was now diminished—and of a different nature. He spent long nostalgic hours indexing his Selkirk pictures; he burned papers and wrote reminiscences for the Dominion Land Surveyor's publication. In 1935 his old chief, Elihu Stewart, died.

Increasingly, he was called upon to write obituaries for the *Canadian Alpine Journal.* His staunch collaborator and friend, Professor Fay, had died in 1931; Professor Coleman in 1938, and Mary Schäffer-Warren in 1939. What memories their passing evoked—the exhilarating Selkirk work, formation of the Alpine Club, climbs and campfires at Robson and Maligne.

He carefully looked over his diaries to write his own obituary. It was a great satisfaction to hear that Oliver had been appointed Surveyor General of India. He immediately sent photos and biographical sketches to major newspapers.

He had a talk with John about his future, urging him to study geology. As a boy, John had wished that there were still frontiers to conquer as there had been in his grandfather's pioneering days. High school science and personal acquaintance with the mountains brought the realization that there *was* pioneering work still to be done. He decided to take his grandfather's advice and devote his career to an understanding of the complex structural development of the mountains. After a distinguished scholastic record at the University of British Columbia, studying geological engineering, and post-graduate work at Columbia University, he joined the Geological Survey of Canada, where Great-Grandfather Macoun had worked.

His first major assignment was a geological survey of the Rogers Pass section of the Selkirk mountains, a task which had to be done before the Trans-Canada highway could be built there. Sixty years before, his grandfather had done the topographical survey.

When A. O. was eighty-one the Club camp was at Rogers Pass, "the Arthur O. Wheeler Camp". John put up his tent and older members happily welcomed and honoured "the Grand Old Man of the Mountains". As the icy air swept down from the glaciers which draped the Selkirks he addressed the annual meeting, wearing—so proudly—his alpine cape and hat. Today the Alpine Club's rustic A. O. Wheeler Memorial Hut nestles in the trees near that campsite.

In 1942 John drove his grandfather to Moraine Lake. A. O. watched the pack-horses moving in long lines to Club camp; he saw happy members tramping up the trails and greeted a few friends, including those good companions of long ago, Swiss guides, Edouard Feuz and Rudolph Aemmer.

In the fall he and Ems celebrated their anniversary over the fire at

"The Grand Old Man of the Mountains."

Claremount and "drank to our healths". He couldn't bring himself to leave the mountains that winter.

They took the train to Golden and spent the bleak months in the little village. On Christmas day they went to the hotel for dinner. Two lonely people amongst six strangers. But the mighty and beloved Selkirks towered across the valley.

On January 9th, 1943 the cable came. Oliver had been knighted. What a spate of letters and telegrams his father sent "re Sir Oliver"!

How proud Mrs. Josephine Helsham Wheeler would have been; the Wheeler honour had been restored in a meaningful way — a knighthood earned for service to Empire.

At home in Sidney in 1943, A.O. cleaned out the office and put up a "for sale" sign. His health was not good; but each morning he brought Ems her tea in bed before returning himself. On May 16th, however, they were off to Banff. Good neighbours and relatives bid them a happy farewell: "Beer all round."

Once again, on the train, he journeyed through the majestic Selkirks; at Banff, "with Ems' good help", he got Claremount in order and fixed Clara's grave.

In July he was in bed, noting in his diary: "Alpine Club Camp opens today." Undoubtedly a few remembered him too — remembered him sitting at the campfire, "the picture of supreme content, his meerschaum in his mouth and the friendly tobacco smoke rising into the night air."

He was alone whem Ems went to the annual meeting of the Skyline Trail Hikers where she presided as President. "All very pleased. Ems did fine as President," he proudly wrote. In October they had an extra fine dinner and "celebrated our anniversary with a bottle of wine." From the windows they watched "the wonderful afterglow of a fiery sunset."

A few days later they took down the Claremount sign. The house wasn't winterized and they moved to a small upstairs flat in a village house.

On Indian summer days he strolled by the Bow, sat in the sun, and smoked his pipe. On October 26th a wire announced the death of the co-founder of the Alpine Club, Elizabeth Parker. In November the snow began falling softly. When he was able to be up and about, he sat by the river and watched happy young couples skating. Did the sights and sounds take him back to gay winter courting days in Collingwood and Ottawa?

He hadn't attended church regularly for years. For him it was true that "on the summits Nature delivers the most eloquent and varied sermons." But now he wrote to the minister of their Sidney church for his "monthly message".

As winter lingered on into March, he wrote his thirty-ninth Annual Anniversary Greetings for Alpine Club Members.

"It is my good fortune to be able to send them from Banff, the home of our headquarters, and as I write, I gaze upon the familiar snow-clad peaks I have known for so long that they are more like old friends than objects of scenic interest: Mounts Cascade, Norquay and the Massive Range on one side; Mounts Peechee, Inglismaldie and Aylmer, the giant guardians of Lake Minnewanka on the other, and to the south stretch the long serrated ridges of Mt. Rundle, Goat and Sulphur Mountains. Bright sunshine, which we have enjoyed almost uninterruptedly since last September, lights up a thin covering of snow and glorifies the scene. Summer or Winter, Canada's Rockies stand unique and without parallel...."

He concluded with a quote "which is surely applicable for the period of war and also to mountain climbing: 'Never give in, *never, never, never* — in nothing, great or small, large or petty—never give in except to convictions of honour and good sense.'"

But time was irrevocably draining the strength from the once powerful body. A few days later he was dead.

Funeral services were held from St. George's in the Pines. According to his wishes he was buried in his Tyrolean cape. the casket was draped in the colours he had used in the design of the Alpine Club crest: green for the earth, grey for the rocks and white for the snow. Crowning it reverently were his Tyrolean hat, ice axe, and climbing rope.

One of the many tributes to him came from L. S. Amery: "In the history of Alpine sport and scientific exploration in the Rockies A. O. Wheeler will always occupy the place that in an earlier generation, men like C. E. Matthews and Tyndall occupied...in the opening up of the Alps. In him long sustained personal achievement and the power of inspiring others, scientific interest and the sheer joy of doing and beholding were blended in a characteristic and irresistibly infectious enthusiasm."

G. Smedley Andrews, formerly Surveyor General of British Columbia, has written: "It has been my good fortune to have climbed some of the mountains in British Columbia....Having climbed to these high stations...I know well the thrill of viewing the august panorama of other peaks circling the horizon. Then on later expeditions...there is the still greater satisfaction of looking backward in grand perspective, on mountains formerly occupied. I can tell you, it is an inspiring experience to scan the rugged horizon and to see here and there peaks that you have known before...and once in a while, far away in the dim distance—recognizing big fellows that you have seen or climbed.

"And so in this world of human affairs, there are certain men who, like grand mountain peaks, rise above the mundane environment to elevations of high eminence in the various fields of human endeavour....How apt are these sentiments in commemorating the professional stature of...Arthur Oliver Wheeler."

Thousands of miles away his noble ancestors lie under fine marble monuments in ancient cathedrals which have withstood the centuries. When they have crumbled to dust, "the Eternal Hills" will still stand guard over the last resting place of the "Grand Old Man of the Mountains."

THE END

Acknowledgements

This biography of A. O. Wheeler would not have been written without the generosity of Dr. John O. Wheeler of Ottawa, who loaned me his grandfather's diaries and papers, and gave me complete freedom to use them as I wished. It is a pleasure to acknowledge my indebtedness to him.

The book would have lacked an essential facet—an understanding of Wheeler's character—without the enthusiastic and competent help of G. Arthur H. Bousfield, of Toronto. He has studied the Wheeler ancestors for years, and provided me with an extensive professional genealogical study, which was enlivened with vivid anecdotes, and the reminiscences of his grandmother, the late Josephine Wheeler Bousfield, youngest sister of A. O. Wheeler. I am happy to express heartfelt gratitude for his interest and very kind assistance.

I wish to thank the Canada Council; a grant under its Canadian Horizons Program made it possible for me to complete my research.

I extend special thanks to A. D. R. Ridge, Provincial Archivist of Alberta, whose institution acted as custodian for the Wheeler papers.

Many relatives, friends, and associates of Mr. Wheeler were most cooperative. I am delighted to express my thanks to: the Macoun family, as represented by Professor Macoun's granddaughters, Mrs. Nora Macoun Wilson and Mrs. Mary Macoun Kennedy, of Ottawa, and Clara Wheeler's niece, Mrs. Eleanor Everall Sanderson, of Victoria; Mr. Wheeler's nieces, Miss Frances Russell Hamilton, of Mississauga, and Mrs. Hester Hughes, of Seattle; Pat Brewster of Banff, Alice Fulmer, Mabel Neville and Sydney Vallance, of Victoria; the late Dr. Fred Bell and Mrs. Marcella Bell of Vancouver, and the late J. N. Wardle of Calgary.

The pleasures of historical research were enhanced by the interest, competence, and friendly cooperation of the staff of Canada's archives where I read early Collingwood, Ottawa, Winnipeg, Calgary, New Westminster, and Banff newspapers, and public documents.

Thanks are also due to Don W. Thomson of Ottawa, author of *Men and Meridians,* who greatly facilitated my work by introducing me to the late Elizabeth Walker, Librarian for the Surveys and Mapping Branch of the National Department of Energy, Mines and Resources. In their Records Room, A. I. Donaldson, located and copied Wheeler's field notebooks and his reports to the Department of the Interior. C. W. Youngs, Director of Surveys, Department of Highways, Government of Alberta, and W. M. Schwartz,

Controller of Surveys for the Province of Saskatchewan's Department of Natural Resources, Lands and Surveys Branch, helped me locate township surveys in their jurisdictions.

My most sincere thanks go to G. Smedley Andrews, Surveyor General of British Columbia, 1952-1968, and Provincial Boundary Commissioner, 1952-1968, who prepared a personal and professional assessment of A. O. Wheeler and his work. He also introduced me to Mr. Wheeler's last surviving assistant, Alan S. (Spike) Thomson, of Victoria, who provided so much valuable information.

I greatly appreciate the cooperation of the Alpine Club of Canada which granted permission to quote extensively from its Journal, and I am grateful to Jeanette Rothrock for generously offering her editorial skills, and to my daughter Linda, for her encouragement, and for typing the manuscript. manuscript.

Photo credits

Alberta Archives: title page, 42, 45, 48, 62, 71, 100, 107, 112, 121, 125, 127, 135, 145, 154

Archives of the Canadian Rockies: 64, 67, 77

Dr. John O. Wheeler: 53, 97, 117, 129

Public Archives: 5, 19, 35, 90

G. Arthur H. Bousfield: 7, 11

Department of the Interior: 105

Index

159

ycis